# Pearson's Canal & River C[ompanion]
## SEVERN & AVON

Published by J. M. Pearson & Son,
Tatenhill Common, Burton-on-Trent,
DE13 9RS.  Telephone (0283) 713674

Second edition 1990.  ISBN 0 907864 54 6

Maps by Malcolm Barnes
Cartographer of Burton upon Trent.

Typeset by Character Graphics
of Taunton, Somerset.

Printed by Penwell of Callington, Cornwall.

# Introduction

THE SEVERN & AVON Canal & River Companion is a practical guide to over a hundred and twenty miles of inland waterways within the counties of Gloucestershire, Worcestershire, Warwickshire and West Midlands. It features the popular AVON RING, a 109 mile circuit comprised of the Lower and Upper Avon Navigations, the Stratford and Worcester & Birmingham canals, and the River Severn. For the average boat crew, the Ring represents around 55 hours cruising; something of a challenge if you attempt to do it in a week, a far more relaxing exploration of some outstanding countryside if you devote a fortnight to it.

However, this guide is equally well suited for use on a wide variety of 'out & back' itineraries. One could devote an unhurried week to the charms of Shakespeare's Avon, or to following the whole of the navigable Severn between Brindley's canal town of Stourport and the old docks at Gloucester, home of the National Waterways Museum. Or perhaps you could try mixing some canal travel with river cruising, comparing the difference in boating techniques and relishing the contrast in the size of the locks. If you don't have a boat of your own, there are seventeen hire bases located beside the waterways covered in this guide; scope enough, surely, for holidays to suite all tastes and schedules.

We also like to think that Pearson's inland waterway guides are of use to non-boaters. Towpath walkers will find them useful because they show clearly the relative condition of the towpath, and whether or not it can be comfortably walked. Details of public transport make 'one-way' walks an easy possibility. Motorists, out for a waterside picnic, or a visit to an old canal or river pub, will find the 'Eating & Drinking' and 'Shopping' details invaluable. Finally, you don't need a boat, a car or a muddy pair of boots at all: the commentary is designed as a narrative entity, and rumour has it that many readers of the Canal Companion series seldom leave the comfort of their armchairs.

The approach to Chadbury Lock, Lower Avon Navigation

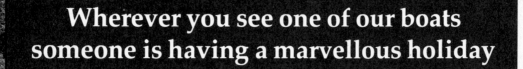

# Wherever you see one of our boats someone is having a marvellous holiday

THERE ARE FOUR River Avons in England. Three are unashamedly West Country waters: one rises on Dartmoor and meets the sea at Salcombe; a second has its source on Salisbury Plain, reaching the English Channel in Poole Bay; the third begins life in the Cotswolds, lends its name to a county, and outpours into the Bristol Channel in dockland surroundings. Each of this trio has its unique character and charm, but none aspires to the beauty and romance of England's other Avon; whether you refer to it as the Warwickshire one, or as Shakespeare's.

By the time this Midland Avon flows into the Severn at Tewkesbury, it has journeyed in excess of a hundred miles from its source on the Northamptonshire Uplands, near the old battlefield of Naseby. For approximately half this distance, between Tewkesbury and Stratford, it is navigable by powered craft. This part of the Avon was first made navigable as long ago as 1639, the work being undertaken by William Sandys of Fladbury at his own expense. During the 18th century separate owners acquired the navigation downstream and upstream of Evesham. Thereafter the river enjoyed mixed fortunes, and with the coming of the railways decay set in; though trade did continue into this century below Pershore.

After the Second World War the Lower Avon was purchased by Douglas Barwell and a trust was formed to restore navigation as far upstream as Evesham, work was completed in 1962. Following re-opening of the Stratford Canal a couple of years later, it became obvious that the missing link – the Upper Avon – should be tackled. The Upper Avon Navigation Trust came into being in 1965 and four years of planning and negotiations ensued before work could begin under the inspirational leadership of David Hutchings. The Upper Avon re-opened in 1974, an astonishing achievement which has few parallels in post war Britain. As David Hutchings is on record as saying, "We were none of us experts, or we should have known it was impossible."

### Navigation Authorities
Lower Avon Navigation Trust, Mill Lane, Wyre Piddle, Pershore, Worcs WR10 2JF Tel: Pershore (0386) 552517.
Upper Avon Navigation Trust, Avon House, Harvington, Evesham, Worcs Tel: Evesham (0386) 870526.

### Maximum Dimensions
Length: 70ft, beam 13½ft, height 10ft, draught 3½ft (4ft on LANT).

### LANT Lock-keeper Telephone Numbers
Avon Lock, Tewkesbury – Tewkesbury (0684) 292129.
Strensham Lock – Evesham (0386) 750355.
Evesham Lock – Evesham (0386) 446511.

Evesham Lock.

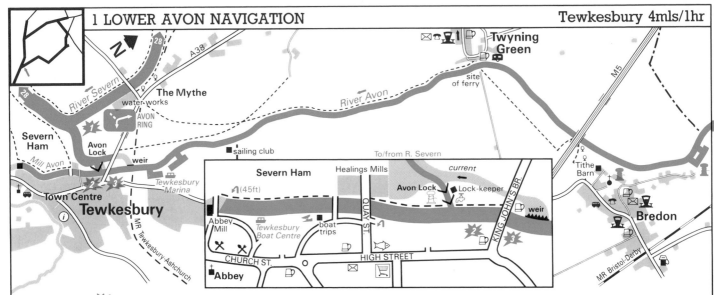

## Navigation Notes

1. Entering or leaving the Avon from or for the Severn it is important to avoid the sandbar. Give this a wide berth by keeping over towards the southern bank as you turn into the Avon, and by making sure that Mythe Bridge is in view before turning upstream into the Severn.
2. Travelling downstream you may have to wait until Avon Lock is free for your use. Try to avoid being taken past the lock entrance by the current, otherwise you may be faced with a difficult manoeuvre to gain access to the chamber.
3. Use the largest arch only at King John's bridge. Visibility is poor, so proceed carefully and use your horn to warn oncoming craft.

## Boating Facilities

TEWKESBURY BOAT CENTRE – St Mary's Lane, Tewkesbury GL20 5SF. Tel: Tewkesbury (0684) 294023. Moorings for cabin cruisers, slipway, boat & engine sales, Calor gas, insurance & finance services, repairs & servicing.
TEWKESBURY MARINA – Bredon Road, Tewkesbury GL20 5BY. Tel: Tewkesbury (0684) 293737. Pumpout, diesel, rubbish & Elsan disposal, repairs & servicing, and chandlery. Moor initially at dock office.

## Moorings

### TEWKESBURY

No free public moorings. We feel that LANT offer the best facilities for which they charge around £1.50 for an overnight stay. These are located on the Mill Avon between Avon Lock and Healing's Mill (you soon get used to the noise of the milling process). Severn Leisure charge £2 for overnight mooring in the channel between King John's bridge and the tail of Avon Lock. Tewkesbury Marina offer moorings by arrangement upstream of King John's bridge and Tewkesbury Boat Centre usually have some space available for small craft on the Mill Avon. Several pubs offer moorings for patrons – see Eating & Drinking.

### TWYNING

Limited facilities by arrangement with the landlord of the "Fleet Inn".

### BREDON

No casual moorings available.

TO THE UNINITIATED, Tewkesbury's waterways appear complex and not a little disconcerting. For instead of being content with one confluence with the Severn, the Avon branches into two channels. The main navigation passes through Avon Lock and meets the Severn below Mythe Bridge. The 'Mill Avon', however, flows between the back of the town and the open pastures of The Ham, being navigable as far as Abbey Mill. Beyond here it is joined by the little River Swilgate for the remainder of the journey to Lower Lode, scene of its second appointment with the Severn.

So, whatever your itinerary, it is likely that Avon Lock will have to be negotiated in one direction or another. It is manned by LANT staff, and operated mechanically while they are on duty. If you are approaching the river for the first time, you will find the lock-keeper a mine of useful information and advice. If, on the other hand, you have come down the river and are about to wave it goodbye, for the time being at least, then take the trouble to say thank you for the help and attention you are likely to have received, from him and his colleagues upstream.

Tewkesbury's riverfront is a delight. So many scenes catch the eye: the ancient arches of King John's bridge; the laid-up grain barges moored against the dusty, redbrick flour mills; the quiet backwaters of the mill stream reflecting half-timbered houses and the town's towering abbey. If you are not already afloat, you can easily arrange to be so, for there are regular trip boats to catch or motor launches to hire.

But the boater can soon leave Tewkesbury's busyness behind. Upstream the Avon is gradually lost in a landscape of water-meadows. How intimate it all seems if you have come from the Severn. How elevated your view of things, now that there are no high banks to hide the outside world. Sailing craft tack to and fro, one moment in Gloucestershire, the next in Worcestershire, because the river forms the boundary between the two counties. The riverside communities of Twyning and Bredon lie on these opposite banks, a mile apart as the crow flies, but half a dozen miles from each other by road now that there is no longer a ferry.

Against the medieval backdrop of Bredon, the motorway intrudes like science fiction, cordoning off the view and filling the environment with noise and fumes. At least you can shift your gaze to the long slate roof of the village's celebrated tithe barn, or the high pitched gables of the manor house; though this is as close as you can get, because there are no casual moorings available in Bredon.

## Tewkesbury

It is feasible to have fallen in love with Tewkesbury without ever having been there, for this is the fact behind the fictional *Elmbury* of John Moore's "Brensham Triology", those glorious post war portraits of a Gloucestershire market town, its surrounding villages and countryside. And if you are familiar with these books, reality – even allowing for the inevitable excesses of road traffic and redevelopment – lets you down gently, because this is an outstanding example of an English country town which, architecturally and atmospherically it would be hard to better. The radiant Abbey of St Mary's looms maternally over the tumbling roofs of tight-knit streets, alleyways and courtyards which lead, at dizzy intervals to tantalizing glimpses of boats moored on the Mill Avon. These alleyways are now an attractive feature of the town, but once they were unspeakably filthy, and in the last century cholera and diphtheria were rife.

### Eating & Drinking

Conscious of its role as a tourist town, Tewkesbury is well endowed with places to eat and drink. Tearooms are thick on the ground; we particularly liked MY GREAT GRANDFATHER'S and MISS MARPLES, both located on Church Street, and both offering early evening meals as well as the usual morning coffees, lunches and afternoon teas. Also in this category is the ABBEY MILL at the far end of the navigable part of the Mill Avon. If you like your food mixed with the sauce of literary associations, then this and the nearby BELL HOTEL deserve your attention, because they were both featured in Mrs Craik's "John Halifax Gentleman". Dickens booked 'Mr Pickwick' into the ROYAL HOP POLE HOTEL which is still generally recognised as Tewkesbury's most prestigious establishment. The front entrance is on Church Street but limited moorings for patrons are located on the Mill Avon. Bar and restaurant meals are always available. Four pubs worth considering are: THE BRITTANIA, a down to earth Davenports house in High Street which does bar lunches; the BERKELEY ARMS, opposite The Cross, a quiet and unspoilt Wadworth pub with a good lunch menu; THE ALBION, situated opposite the Roses Theatre (where the comedian Eric Morecambe died), which does Halls beers and food both sessions; and finally, back beside the river, THE BLACK BEAR which has customer moorings beside King John's Bridge; it dates back to the 14th century, families are welcome, food is usually available and the beer is Flowers.

### Shopping

Tewkesbury is a country market town par excellence with some splendid butchers, bakers and – no, not candle stick makers, but – delicatessens. Not surprisingly there are some excellent gift shops, antique dealers, and bookshops. There is a National Trust shop in one of the Abbey Lawns medieval cottages. Some shops draw their blinds and close early on a Thursday. The market is held on Wednesdays and Saturdays.

### Things to Do

TOURIST INFORMATION CENTRE/MUSEUM – Barton Street. Tel: Tewkesbury (0684) 295027. Open daily, Apr-Oct. Friendly and helpful ladies to point you in all the right directions. small admission charge for adjoining museum of local history.

JOHN MOORE COUNTRYSIDE MUSEUM – Church Street. Tel: Tewkesbury (0684) 297174. Small admission charge. Open Tue-Sat. Excellent little museum housed in 15th century half-timbered cottage. Celebrates the life and works of the town's local author, reflecting his love of the surrounding countryside.

*continued on page 60*

THE LOWER AVON seems obsessed by Bredon Hill, never letting it out of its sight, fascinated by the summit's constantly changing shape. Half wooded, half bare, like mottled baize, it forms an island between the Cotswold Edge and the distant serrated outline of the Malvern Hills. Because its peak falls short of a thousand feet, some 18th century eccentric built a folly on its top so that he could stand that high above sea level. But what's a few feet here or there in countryside as delectable as this. Each entertaining curve in the Avon reveals a new perspective, like falling deeper and deeper in love with someone who is going to mean a lot to you.

This Avon is second only to the Thames in the amount of writing it has inspired, and this stretch is particularly rich in literary associations. Every guidebook quotes A.E. Housman's poem "In Summertime on Bredon" (a peculiar topographical aberration for a set of poems entitled "A Shropshire Lad"), but a better poem was written by Sir Arthur Quiller-Couch about Eckington Bridge. 'Q' had canoed the river as a young man in 1890, and had been inspired to write a magnificent ode to the bridge, which speaks of "eloquent grooves worn into the sandstone by labouring bargemen". Quiller-Couch also used the river in his adventurous tale of "True Tilda", painting a particularly evocative scene of the bustling barges and steam tugs at Tewkesbury. Following his own journey down the river in 1910,

Temple Thurston used Nafford Mill as the setting for his Richard Furlong trilogy; now long-forgotten and out of print, but still wonderful reading if you can find them, as it is reasonably easy to do, second-hand. It is not difficult to see why such writers were moved to capture the spirit of this quintessentially English landscape. It would be remise of you not to moor (at Comberton Quay or Eckington Bridge) and make the ascent of Bredon to see Housman's 'coloured counties' for yourself, and *your* river meandering from village to village like a wandering minstrel.

Strensham Lock is manned and automated. Subconsciously the name conjures images of smelly loos and stodgy food, but a church-topped hill hides the river from the motorway service area, and either side of the lock the river roams attractively past shallow banks of reeds and lily-pads rutted by cattle intent on quenching their thirst. Downstream of Eckington's medieval bridge, in a reach used by sailing craft from the Arden club, the busy Bristol – Derby railway crosses the river by way of a not ungraceful iron span resting on stone piers. It comes as something of a surprise to learn that Herbert Spencer, the great Victorian philosopher, was instrumental in its design during his youthful sojourn in the engineering offices of the Birmingham & Gloucester Railway Company.

**Eckington**
A pleasant, if unremarkable vegetable growing village half a mile to the south of the glorious bridge which bears its name. Three pubs, post office, general store open daily (inc Sun am) and butcher. Can also be reached by lane from Strensham Lock.

**Birlingham**
Back of beyond village almost islanded by the Avon. Can be reached by footpath from Nafford Lock. One quiet pub and a telephone kiosk.

**Great Comberton**
Sleepy village with no facilities other than a telephone. Access, however, from Comberton Quay to the summit of Bredon Hill.

The Swan's Neck.

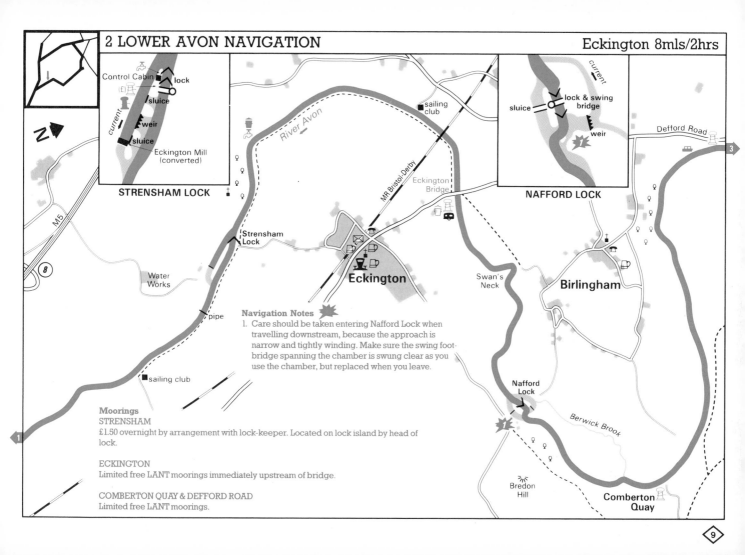

**STRENSHAM LOCK**

Control Cabin
lock
(£)
sluice
current
weir
sluice
Eckington Mill
(converted)

**NAFFORD LOCK**

current
lock & swing
bridge
sluice
weir

N

River Avon

sailing
club

Strensham
Lock

M5

Eckington

Eckington
Bridge

MR Bristol-Derby

Water
Works

Swan's
Neck

Birlingham

Defford Road

3

pipe

**Navigation Notes**

1. Care should be taken entering Nafford Lock when travelling downstream, because the approach is narrow and tightly winding. Make sure the swing foot-bridge spanning the chamber is swung clear as you use the chamber, but replaced when you leave.

sailing club

Nafford
Lock

Berwick Brook

**Moorings**

STRENSHAM
£1.50 overnight by arrangement with lock-keeper. Located on lock island by head of lock.

ECKINGTON
Limited free LANT moorings immediately upstream of bridge.

COMBERTON QUAY & DEFFORD ROAD
Limited free LANT moorings.

Bredon
Hill

Comberton
Quay

1

8

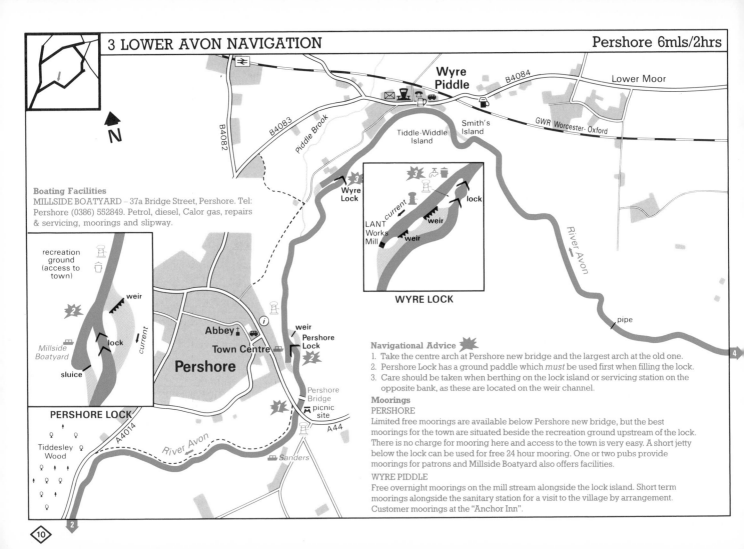

Lower Moor

Wyre Piddle

Tiddle-Widdle Island

Smith's Island

GWR Worcester- Oxford

River Avon

Wyre Lock

pipe

## Boating Facilities

MILLSIDE BOATYARD – 37a Bridge Street, Pershore. Tel: Pershore (0386) 552849. Petrol, diesel, Calor gas, repairs & servicing, moorings and slipway.

recreation ground (access to town)

weir

**WYRE LOCK**

LANT Works Mill

current

weir

weir

lock

Millside Boatyard

lock

current

sluice

**PERSHORE LOCK**

Pershore

Abbey

Town Centre

weir

Pershore Lock

Tiddesley Wood

A4014

River Avon

Pershore Bridge

picnic site

A44

Sanders

## Navigational Advice

1. Take the centre arch at Pershore new bridge and the largest arch at the old one.
2. Pershore Lock has a ground paddle which *must* be used first when filling the lock.
3. Care should be taken when berthing on the lock island or servicing station on the opposite bank, as these are located on the weir channel.

## Moorings

### PERSHORE

Limited free moorings are available below Pershore new bridge, but the best moorings for the town are situated beside the recreation ground upstream of the lock. There is no charge for mooring here and access to the town is very easy. A short jetty below the lock can be used for free 24 hour mooring. One or two pubs provide moorings for patrons and Millside Boatyard also offers facilities.

### WYRE PIDDLE

Free overnight moorings on the mill stream alongside the lock island. Short term moorings alongside the sanitary station for a visit to the village by arrangement. Customer moorings at the "Anchor Inn".

THE VALE OF EVESHAM is at its most beguiling as the Avon wanders past the town of Pershore. Pollarded willows and swaying poplars etch out the river's course across the valley floor towards the thick-set tower of Pershore Abbey.

The original bridge at PERSHORE dates from the 14th century and contrives to look even older. Military men have always had a love hate relationship with bridges, and the Cavaliers tried to demolish this one as they escaped from the Battle of Worcester in 1651. Thankfully it stood its ground. Seemingly nothing could mar the charm of its setting or its own inherent beauty. Nothing that is, until the motor car came along, demanding construction of a straighter, flater span. Built in 1928, it was, they boasted, the first concrete bridge in Worcestershire. Nothing to be proud of chaps, nothing at all.

Pershore Mill was destroyed by fire early in the 1970s. It was the last mill on the river to remain in commercial use. It was also the source of the Avon's last barge traffic, a little barge with the biblically appropriate name of *Pisgah* traded to and from the mill until the end.

WYRE LOCK is diamond shaped, and though hand operated, is often worked by volunteers. Collecting boxes are displayed at the manned locks on the Lower Avon and it's worth having a supply of pound coins to hand, for though donations are not actively sought, loose change is a small price to pay for the unfunded upkeep of such a lovely waterway. Many of the original Avon locks were of unusual shape to reduce erosion of the chambers by the force of water from the sluices. LANT's offices are located here and the old mill – said to be the ugliest on the river, though it looked pretty nice to us – is used as a social and sailing club by LANT members.

Desirable residences create an enviable riverside environment for the villagers of WYRE PIDDLE. Well groomed gardens spill down to the riverbank where substantial cruisers are moored, status symbols of an affluence which, once attained, has an ironic capacity for losing its appeal. How seldom boats like this seem to be used. They lie at their moorings, waiting perhaps for their owners to make some symbolic gesture of escape, a way out of the morass of middle class conventions and routines that their wealth has created for them. At least someone *has* made good *their* escape to the house on stilts, hidden among the trees on Smith's Island, where they can fantasise for themselves a Swiss Family Robinson existence beyond the grip of the rat race. Upstream of here the river loses itself amongst the fruit fields and orchards of its fertile valley, herons and kingfishers abound, and time hangs motionlessly over the landscape like the cobwebby pendulum of an unwound grandfather clock.

## Pershore

Pershore is generally regarded as the model for *Borchester* in the Radio Four serial 'The Archers'; though you are probably safe to walk its streets without bumping into Nigel Pargeter or Eddie Grundy. It's a lovely little town, couched in the shadow of Bredon Hill. Balconies blossoming from Georgian houses lend a holiday feel, an inherent *joie d'vivre* to Pershore, best known nowadays, not for pears as its name implies, but for rich red ruby plums. The Abbey, only marginally less imposing than Tewkesbury's, was partially demolished following the Dissolution of the Monastries. John Betjeman wrote of the Abbey bells being rung for evensong in his poem, "Pershore Station". Boaters are afforded easy access to the town, across playing fields and past an impressive leisure complex, to the quaint and bustling indoor market.

### Eating & Drinking

THE ANGEL INN – High Street. Old posting inn recommended by Les Routiers. Lunches, teas, dinners and bar snacks.

MILLERS ARMS – Bridge Street. Quaint Wadworth pub. Bar meals both sessions, children catered for.
THE STAR HOTEL – Bridge Street. Customer moorings above Pershore Lock. Bar and restaurant meals.

### Shopping

Shopping is generally a more agreeable experience here as opposed to frenetic Evesham. The indoor retail market operates on Wednesdays, Fridays and Saturdays. Elsewhere there are lots of interesting little shops tucked down alleyways or in quiet courtyards away from the hullabaloo of High Street. Several antique shops plus new and antiquarian bookshops.

### Things to Do

TOURIST INFORMATION CENTRE – Council Offices, High Street. Tel: Pershore (0386) 554711.
Motor launches can be hired from J. SANDERS boatyard situated downstream of Pershore Bridge. Tel: Pershore (0386) 552765.

### Public Transport

BUSES – Midland Red West to/from Worcester & Evesham. no Sunday service. Tel: (0345) 212555. Local 'Plumline' minibus connection with railway station – see below.
TRAINS – 'Cotswold Line' services to/from Worcester, Hereford, Evesham & Oxford. Tel: Worcester (0905) 27211.

## Wyre Piddle

Straggling riverside village on the road between Pershore and Evesham. The POST OFFICE STORES sells groceries, newspapers, wines & spirits, but doesn't open at all on Sundays. THE ANCHOR is arguably the Avon's pleasantest inn. A well piled quay makes mooring easy for patrons and there's a wide and excellent choice of bar and restaurant food. The beer is Flowers and there are nice views from the precipitous garden out across the river towards Bredon Hill.

**H**ISTORICALLY, EVESHAM MARKS the frontier between the Lower and Upper navigable sections of the River Avon. Between Cropthorne and Offenham the river practically boxes the compass on its gorgeous meanderings through the fruity vale.

In the nineteenth century the only way to cross the river at CROPTHORNE was to ford it. But in Queen Victoria's Jubilee year a bridge was built to span the river here, so that Fladbury lads could go courting Cropthorne lasses without necessarily getting their feet wet. If you are American and 'in to' word association, you might jump from Ford to Nixon, and naturally from Nixon to Watergate. The Avon had its 'water- gates' too, and one of the last stood below Jubilee Bridge. They were devices for altering water levels without affecting supplies to the mills. A conventional lock here would have probably have lowered the water level to the detriment of the mill at Wyre. The water-gate provided a simple alternative. It consisted of a gate fitted with sluices set into a weir. In normal circumstances the gate would remain open until a boat passed through on its way upstream. Then the gate would be closed and the boat would wait for a sufficient level of water to be built up to enable it to pass navigate up to Fladbury Lock. On the way back the sluices would be drawn once the boat had reached the gate, and there it would wait until the levels had equalised once more and the gate could be opened.

The Avon at FLADBURY is extraordinarily beautiful. There were two mills here, that beside the lock being known as Cropthorne Mill in deference to its position near the east bank of the river. In "The Flower of Gloster" Temple Thurston thought it would be a wonderful place to be a child in. We watched a boy, a girl and a dog set off on an adventure in a rowing boat like something out of Arthur Ransome, and met a teenage girl with flame red hair fishing insouciantly at the tail of the lock, a latter-day Anne of Green Gables, apparently indifferent to the platitudes of pop and the fripperies of fashion which so engross most girls of her age.

The rhyming locks at Fladbury and Chadbury deserve a poem about them. Certainly there is plenty of inspiration in the landscape as the river winds past the orcharded flanks of Craycombe and Wood Norton hills. Craycombe House was built for George Perrott, an 18th century owner of the navigation. The novelist Francis Brett Young lived in it for a while during the Thirties. Wood Norton house is used by the BBC as a training centre, but once belonged to the Duke of Orleans, a pretender to the French throne. Like most Avon mills, the one at Chadbury has been converted into a private dwelling. Very nice too, but how one aches to see an Avon mill in business again, doing the job it was built to do, at no cost to the environment. It would be viable too, given the tourist trade and the demand for stone ground wholemeal flour. CHADBURY LOCK was the first to be rebuilt by LANT in 1953. Much of the work was done by the the Royal Engineers, a pioneering use of military resources on a civilian project.

Above the tree tops bordering the next reach stands the Leicester Tower, built in 1840 as a memorial to Simon de Montfort, the Earl of Leicester, who came a cropper at the Battle of Evesham in 1265. The monks of Evesham Abbey planted vineyards on these south facing slopes in the middle ages. Round the corner two railway bridges spanned the river. One remains, carrying the scenic 'Cotswold Line' on its way from Worcester to Oxford. The abandoned line formed a roundabout route between Gloucester and

*continued on page 59*

## Navigational Advice

1. Cruising upstream keep left below Jubilee Bridge; downstream, keep right.
2. The southern approach to/exit from Fladbury Lock is too narrow to pass oncoming craft; proceed with care.
3. Approach Hampton ferry with caution. The ferry rope will need to be submerged for you to pass. Sound your horn three times to alert the ferryman of your presence and proceed very slowly.
4. Beware shallows on outside of bend downstream of confluence with River Isbourne.
5. Use centre arch in either direction at Workman Bridge.

## Moorings

### CROPTHORNE & FLADBURY

The house on the east bank, immediately downstream of Jubilee Bridge, provides the only convenient moorings for these villages. Current charges are £1 during the day and £2 overnight.

### CRAYCOMBE TURN

Free LANT moorings but no access to outside world.

### EVESHAM

The local authority provide moorings downstream of Workman Bridge. There's room here for about 6 average length hire boats, though people are usually happy to double-up at busy times. Water and refuse disposal facilities are laid on as well. Daytime mooring is free, but they charge for overnight stays. Just downstream is a small free LANT 24 hour mooring. To our mind the *best* moorings in Evesham are to be had upstream of the lock. LANT charge £1.50 per night here, but it's a much quieter spot than Workman Gardens.

### OFFENHAM

Limited moorings at the pub.

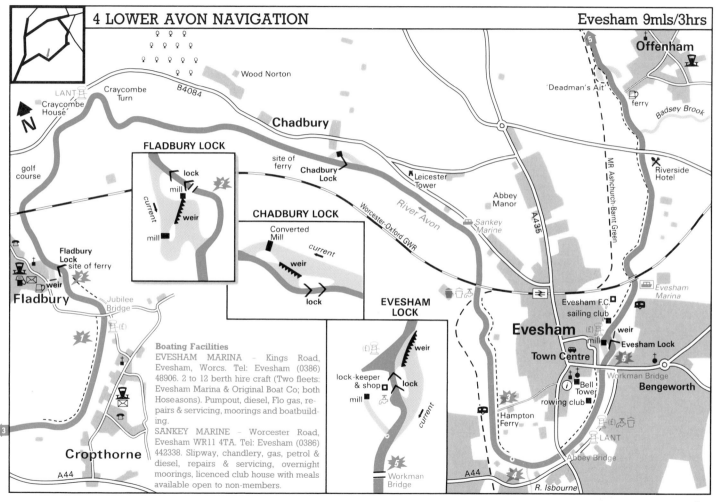

Wood Norton

B4084

Craycombe Turn

LANT

Craycombe House

Chadbury

N

golf course

**FLADBURY LOCK**

lock

mill

current

weir

mill

2

site of ferry

Chadbury Lock

Leicester Tower

Abbey Manor

River Avon

Sankey Marine

A435

Offenham

'Deadman's Ait'

ferry

Badsey Brook

MR Ashchurch-Barnt Green

Riverside Hotel

Worcester-Oxford GWR

**CHADBURY LOCK**

Converted Mill

weir

current

lock

**EVESHAM LOCK**

lock-keeper & shop

mill

weir

lock

current

Evesham Marina

Evesham F.C. sailing club

weir

mill

Evesham Lock

5

**Evesham**

Town Centre

Bell Tower

rowing club

i

Workman Bridge

Bengeworth

Fladbury Lock

site of ferry

weir

**Fladbury**

Jubilee Bridge

(£)

2

1

3

**Cropthorne**

A44

### Boating Facilities

EVESHAM MARINA – Kings Road, Evesham, Worcs. Tel: Evesham (0386) 48906. 2 to 12 berth hire craft (Two fleets: Evesham Marina & Original Boat Co; both Hoseasons). Pumpout, diesel, Flo gas, repairs & servicing, moorings and boatbuilding.

SANKEY MARINE – Worcester Road, Evesham WR11 4TA. Tel: Evesham (0386) 442338. Slipway, chandlery, gas, petrol & diesel, repairs & servicing, overnight moorings, licenced club house with meals available open to non-members.

Workman Bridge

5

Hampton Ferry

3

LANT

Abbey Bridge

A44

R. Isbourne

4

13

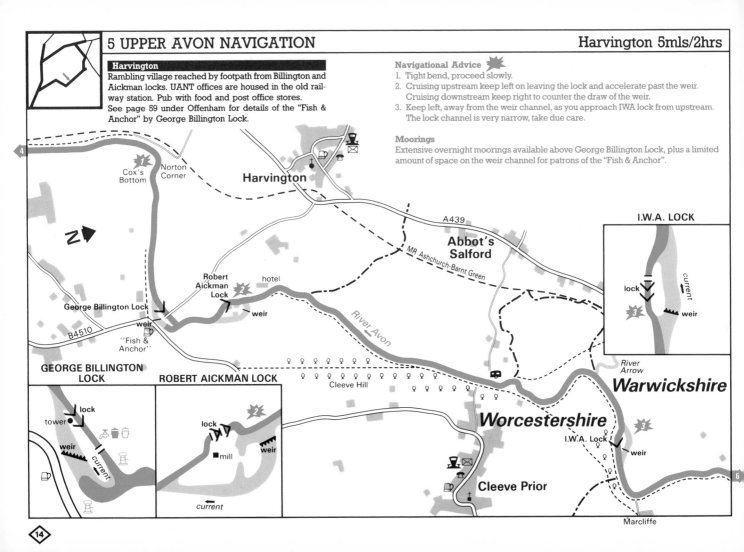

### Harvington

Rambling village reached by footpath from Billington and Aickman locks. UANT offices are housed in the old railway station. Pub with food and post office stores. See page 59 under Offenham for details of the "Fish & Anchor" by George Billington Lock.

### Navigational Advice

1. Tight bend, proceed slowly.
2. Cruising upstream keep left on leaving the lock and accelerate past the weir. Cruising downstream keep right to counter the draw of the weir.
3. Keep left, away from the weir channel, as you approach IWA lock from upstream. The lock channel is very narrow, take due care.

### Moorings

Extensive overnight moorings available above George Billington Lock, plus a limited amount of space on the weir channel for patrons of the "Fish & Anchor".

Cox's Bottom

Norton Corner

**Harvington**

A439

MR Ashchurch-Barnt Green

**Abbot's Salford**

**I.W.A. LOCK**

lock — current

weir

River Arrow

**Warwickshire**

Robert Aickman Lock

hotel

weir

George Billington Lock

weir

B4510

"Fish & Anchor"

River Avon

Cleeve Hill

**Worcestershire**

I.W.A. Lock

weir

**GEORGE BILLINGTON LOCK**

lock

tower

weir — current

**ROBERT AICKMAN LOCK**

lock

weir

mill

current

**Cleeve Prior**

Marcliffe

UNCANNILY, THE AVON seems to sense the change in navigation authority which takes place at Evesham. Upstream of the sharp bend at NORTON CORNER the river is both narrower and shallower, and box-hulled narrowboats doing The Ring in an anti-clockwise direction, lose the unaccustomed sense of gay abandon they've enjoyed since Worcester. With the exception of Luddington, Upper Avon locks are named after individuals or groups associated with the restoration of navigation. ROBERT AICKMAN LOCK commemorates one of the most influential figures of the post war inland waterways renaissance. Aickman founded the Inland Waterways Association in 1946 and crusaded for the waterways cause for a further twenty years. Bringing navigation back to the Avon was one of the projects which gave him most delight, and he was on the council of both Trusts. A memorial plaque, set in an attractive sweep of brickwork, graces the lockside, paying homage to his achievements and single-minded dedication.

Quiller-Couch wrote of 'clouds of sweet-smelling flour' issuing from the doorway of Cleeve Mill, but virtually all trace of the lock, weir and mill at CLEEVE has vanished. At the turn of the century, indeed up until the second world war, this was a popular venue for picnics. You could get cream teas at the mill, and hire a skiff for a leisurely row on the river. The Avon broadened below the weir and was shallow enough to be crossed by the hay carts at harvest time. At the foot of its wooded escarpment, the setting is still seductive, but somewhat marred by the presence of a caravan park on the Warwickshire bank, and by the lack of access for boaters to the pretty village of Cleeve itself.

Downstream of the IWA LOCK, the River Arrow has its confluence with the Avon. Sandys considered making part of this navigable, but obviously never got around to it. The Arrow rises on the Lickey Hills and passes through the lower reservoir at Bittell beside the Worcester & Birmingham Canal, so you may well see it again. Likewise its tributary, the Alne, which follows the Stratford Canal for a while in the vicinity of Preston Bagot. Marlcliffe is aptly named, for the Trust had considerable problems during the construction of the IWA lock, due to the unyielding quality of the marl substrata. UANT's handbook and guide describes many of the difficulties overcome during the restoration in a matter of a fact way. A modesty which fails to disguise the vast amount of work they undertook, and still undertake on our behalf.

Bidford - on - Avon.

THE UPPER AVON is at its loveliest between Bidford and Weston. Locks come at satisfying intervals, but the rest of the time you have every justification for just sitting back and watching the peaceful landscape slip uneventfully astern. Neither is it absolutely necessary to be afloat to enjoy the seclusion of this part of the river, because an excellent public footpath stretches from Marlcliffe (Map 5) through Bidford to Stratford (Map 7), allowing those on foot to see more than just a tantalising glimpse of the river for once.

BIDFORD positively bristles with boats, coming in to moor with varying degrees of proficiency, or threading their way gingerly through the single and narrow navigation arch of the 15th century bridge. Old cronies gossip on the cutwaters, enjoying a private joke or two at the expense of the less adept boaters, or eyeing with obvious relish the amount of flesh exposed by female boaters on hot days.

The Romans chose to cross the Avon at Bidford. Their Ryknild Street forded the river here on its way to the town of Alcester. Later the road was known as Buckle Street, and it was the monks of Alcester who built the present bridge which dates from 1482. None of its seven arches are alike in size or shape, and it still looks so medieval, that the regular passage across its narrow span of a Midland Red double-decker, looks quite anachronistic.

UANT's locks are not always situated in exact accordance with those on the original navigation. For instance, E & H Billington and Pilgrim locks are located either side of the former lock at Bidford Grange. Similarly, there used to be two separate locks at Welford which UANT have replaced by the single W.A. Cadbury lock. These changes were necessitated by the alteration of water levels in the intervening years between dereliction of the original navigation and the commencement of work on the new scheme in the early Seventies. The attitudes of landowners, local and water authorities also had its influence on the final shape of the UANT project. Sometimes such individuals and bodies were extraordinarily helpful, whilst others

seemed determined to stop the scheme in its tracks. Inexplicably, and as Robert Aickman put it, the restorers were not always seen to be on the side of the angels.

The reputedly haunted manor house at HILLBOROUGH overlooks the remote reach between Pilgrim and Cadbury locks. The Merry Monarch hid here whilst on the run from his defeat at the Battle of Worcester in 1651. It is said that he left some treasure behind at Hillborough in his hurry to escape. If he did, it has never been known to have been found. But then would you tell anyone if you discovered a treasure trove?

The river splits into several channels – only one of which is navigable – to pass beneath the ancient arches of BINTON BRIDGES. Nearby lies the trackbed of the old Stratford & Midland Junction Railway, one of those endearingly independant cross country lines which seemed to lead from nowhere to nowhere. At plum-picking time up to twenty wagons a day were loaded with fruit in the tiny siding at Binton. The line's most important trains were the 'banana specials', operated by the Midland Railway between Avonmouth Docks and London, in roundabout rivalry with the Great Western.

### Moorings
**BIDFORD**
Good length of free moorings on southern, recreation ground bank downstream of bridge. One or two pubs on the opposite bank have moorings by arrangement with patrons.
Elsewhere, there are limited 24 hour moorings on the lock islands between Bidford and Binton, but no access to/from the outside world.

**BINTON**
Good length of long and short term moorings available at Welford Boat Station. Overnight charges vary according to length of boat. Limited moorings available at "The Four Alls".

### Bidford-on-Avon
There's a resort like air about Bidford. Day trippers use the riverside recreation ground as a car park but rarely stray much further than the local pubs and cafes. Moreover such indulgences fail to mar what is an otherwise attractive village. In any case, Shakespeare came here to drink too, immortalising the place as by referring to it as 'drunken Bidford' in one of his poems.

**Eating & Drinking**
Wide range of pubs (try the ANGLO SAXON), restaurants, tea rooms and fish & chip shops.

**Shopping**
Good choice of shops. Nice little bookshop. Lloyds bank up by church.

**Public Transport**
BUSES – Midland Red South to/from Evesham and Stratford. Tel: Rugby (0788) 535555.

### Welford-on-Avon
Not to be confused with the *other* Welford-on-Avon way upstream in Leicestershire, near the river's source on Naseby Field, this Welford is notable for its maypole and

some pretty thatched cottages. There is no access to the village from Cadbury Lock, so boaters must approach it from Binton Bridges.

**Eating & Drinking**
THE FOUR ALLS – riverside at Binton Bridges. A plush Whitbread 'Wayside Inn'. Families catered for. Two other nice pubs in the village.

**Shopping**
Post office stores, general store (with off licence) and butcher.

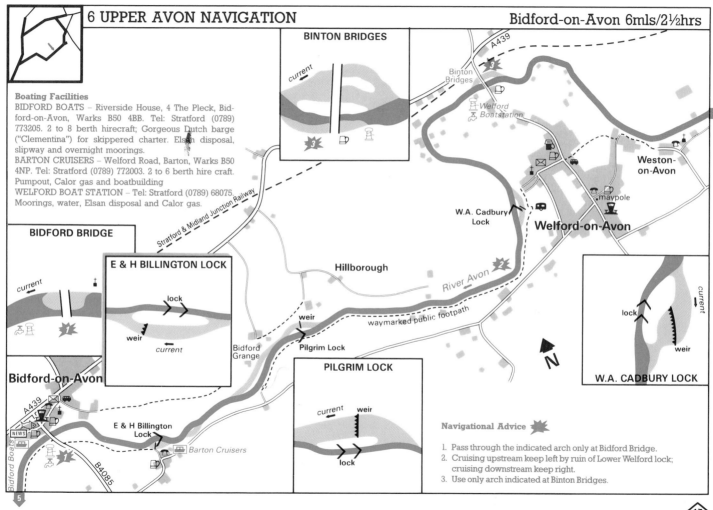

## BINTON BRIDGES

current

## Boating Facilities

BIDFORD BOATS – Riverside House, 4 The Pleck, Bidford-on-Avon, Warks B50 4BB. Tel: Stratford (0789) 773205. 2 to 8 berth hirecraft; Gorgeous Dutch barge ("Clementina") for skippered charter. Elsan disposal, slipway and overnight moorings.

BARTON CRUISERS – Welford Road, Barton, Warks B50 4NP. Tel: Stratford (0789) 772003. 2 to 6 berth hire craft. Pumpout, Calor gas and boatbuilding

WELFORD BOAT STATION – Tel: Stratford (0789) 68075. Moorings, water, Elsan disposal and Calor gas.

A439

Binton Bridges

Welford Boatstation

Weston-on-Avon

maypole

Welford-on-Avon

W.A. Cadbury Lock

Stratford & Midland Junction Railway

## BIDFORD BRIDGE

current

## E & H BILLINGTON LOCK

lock

weir

current

Hillborough

River Avon

waymarked public footpath

weir

Bidford Grange

Pilgrim Lock

Bidford-on-Avon

A439

NEWS

E & H Billington Lock

Barton Cruisers

Bidford Boats

B4085

## PILGRIM LOCK

current

weir

lock

## W.A. CADBURY LOCK

lock

current

weir

N

### Navigational Advice

1. Pass through the indicated arch only at Bidford Bridge.
2. Cruising upstream keep left by ruin of Lower Welford lock; cruising downstream keep right.
3. Use only arch indicated at Binton Bridges.

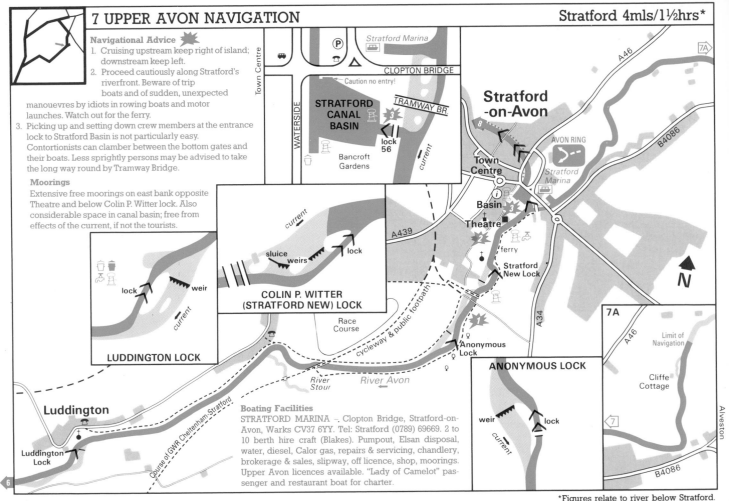

**Navigational Advice**

1. Cruising upstream keep right of island; downstream keep left.
2. Proceed cautiously along Stratford's riverfront. Beware of trip boats and of sudden, unexpected manouevres by idiots in rowing boats and motor launches. Watch out for the ferry.
3. Picking up and setting down crew members at the entrance lock to Stratford Basin is not particularly easy. Contortionists can clamber between the bottom gates and their boats. Less sprightly persons may be advised to take the long way round by Tramway Bridge.

**Moorings**

Extensive free moorings on east bank opposite Theatre and below Colin P. Witter lock. Also considerable space in canal basin; free from effects of the current, if not the tourists.

Town Centre

WATERSIDE

Stratford Marina

CLOPTON BRIDGE

Caution no entry!

STRATFORD CANAL BASIN

TRAMWAY BR.

3

lock 56

current

Bancroft Gardens

Stratford -on-Avon

A46

7A

8

AVON RING

B4086

Town Centre

Stratford Marina

i

Basin Theatre

3

current

sluice

weirs

lock

A439

2

ferry

Stratford New Lock

**COLIN P. WITTER (STRATFORD NEW) LOCK**

lock

weir

current

**LUDDINGTON LOCK**

Race Course

cycleway & public footpath

1

Anonymous Lock

A34

**ANONYMOUS LOCK**

weir

lock

current

7A

Limit of Navigation

A46

Cliffe Cottage

7

B4086

Alveston

Luddington

River Stour

River Avon

Luddington Lock

Course of GWR Cheltenham-Stratford

N

**Boating Facilities**

STRATFORD MARINA –, Clopton Bridge, Stratford-on-Avon, Warks CV37 6YY. Tel: Stratford (0789) 69669. 2 to 10 berth hire craft (Blakes). Pumpout, Elsan disposal, water, diesel, Calor gas, repairs & servicing, chandlery, brokerage & sales, slipway, off licence, shop, moorings. Upper Avon licences available. "Lady of Camelot" passenger and restaurant boat for charter.

6

*Figures relate to river below Stratford.

THE UPPER AVON winds from Luddington, past Stratford, to the head of navigation at Alveston Weir. Boaters have three river locks to contend with, plus a fourth if they are moving onto or off the canal at Stratford.

The old Upper Lock at LUDDINGTON had a circular chamber. Just over a mile upstream the River Stour enters the Avon. It rises high up on the Cotswolds near the famous brewery at Hook Norton. Above the confluence a large steel girder bridge carries the trackbed of the Great Western line between Stratford and Cheltenham. The line was lifted around 1980 and has been converted into a cycleway. Nearby is Stratford Race Course.

ANONYMOUS LOCK commemorates all those who donated funds towards restoration of the Upper Avon. The Queen Mother travelled from here to Stratford Lock by narrowboat during the opening ceremonies of June 1st, 1974.

The short reach separating Anonymous and Stratford locks is crossed by the Stratford & Midland Junction Railway bridge which has been converted to carry a road. A footbridge also spans the river at this point, making it easy for pedestrians to walk down one bank from the town centre and return by the other. Blocks of flats have replaced Lucy's Mill which stood here for hundreds of years, being an important customer of the river barges until the advent of the railway.

Stratford New Lock was renamed COLIN P. WITTER LOCK in 1986. Massive steel frames protect the chamber from collapse threatened by high ground pressures. The bold steeple of Holy Trinity Church (Shakespeare's burial place) overlooks the lock. Just upstream operates the Avon's second remaining ferry boat, using a submerged chain fed through a winch on the pontoon, wound by the ferryman.

STRATFORD'S riverfront is familiar to people from all over the world. If they haven't seen it for themselves, they'll have seen it on chocolate box lids, or table mats, or on the sort of calendars which hang in dentist's waiting rooms above the fish tank. But if the view is hackneyed it can still

entrance. And if you are not already afloat, there is no excuse for not getting so. Motor launch or rowing boat hire is easy, and trip boats ply between the lock and Clopton Bridge. If you have had the benefit of an Oxbridge education there are even punts to be hired from the Boathouse on the east bank above Tramway Bridge. We watched three sikhs in full costume set uncertainly off in a motor launch, transforming Shakespeare's Avon, for one marvellously incongruous moment into a tributary of the Ganges.

Upstream of the entrance lock to Stratford Basin, the river is spanned by TRAMWAY BRIDGE, a redbrick structure built in 1826 to carry the Stratford & Moreton Horse Tramway. It is now used by pedestrians. In contrast, the stone arches of CLOPTON BRIDGE date back to 1480, but the two bridges harmonise well with their shared environment, as though the gap of four centuries in their construction was just a twinkling ripple in the timespan of the river beneath them.

Beyond Stratford the Avon is currently navigable for another couple of uneventful miles or so as far as ALVESTON. Plans were published in the early Eighties to extend navigation upstream as far as Warwick, where a link could be made with the Grand Union Canal. Three-quarters of the route is already deemed to be navigable; a couple of weirs and half a dozen locks would complete the job. But the scheme foundered on the rocky attitudes of riparian landowners, reluctant to countenance the passage of pleasure boats through the privacy of their water-meadows. Strange then, that the same individuals should do nothing to prevent construction of the Oxford – Birmingham motorway across the same landscape. But it would be churlish to leave the Avon on such a sour note. Boating enthusiasts and holidaymakers have fifty miles of gorgeous river to play with thanks to the imagination and graft of the two Trusts and their volunteers. The other ten miles to Warwick is something to look forward to in years to come. Attitudes and personalities change, the river can bide its time.

## Stratford-on-Avon

That Stratford is second only to London in the esteem of foreign visitors, serves to emphasise the charisma surrounding Shakespeare. Without his omnipresence one imagines Stratford's position in the league tables of tourism would be accademic. And yet, subtract the Shakespeare factor, and you are still left with an attractive town with its fair share of good architecture; its setting enhanced by the proximity of the Avon. Contriving a dramatic analogy, Stratford delivers its lines and plays its part, yet survives with its integrity intact, really being the rather nice place to visit as extolled by the tourist propaganda.

### Eating & Drinking
ARDEN HOTEL – Waterside. Bar and restaurant meals. Gorgeous open air patio for coffees, lunches and teas on hot summer days.
THE BOATHOUSE – adjacent Tramway Bridge on opposite bank from canal basin. Wine bar.

THE DIRTY DUCK – adjacent to Swan Theatre on Waterside. Flowers ales, bar and restaurant meals.
HATHAWAYS – High Street. Timeless tea rooms.
RICHOUX – Old Red Lion Court, off Bridge Street. Branch of famous London patisserie.
WATER RAT – riverside (south bank). Cafe and brasserie.
The foregoing is the briefest selection: three restaurants also worth trying: THE VINTNER, BOBBY BROWNS and THE OPPOSITION; all in Sheep Street.

continued on page 60.

Edstone Aqueduct.

**T**HE STRATFORD-UPON-AVON CANAL holds a special place in the affections of a whole generation of canal enthusiasts. Its southern section was the first great restoration success story of the post war canal movement; being transformed from near total dereliction, and the threat of abandonment in 1958, to navigable status once again in 1964. This pioneering transformation, under the inspired leadership of Midlands architect David Hutchings, blazed a trail which subsequent canal restoration projects, such as the Kennet & Avon, Montgomery and Basingstoke schemes, have sought to follow. Perhaps the most telling statistic related to its rescue, is that restoration cost virtually half the figure quoted for abandonment. A chastening thought, probably lost on those bodies responsible for the loss of so much canal mileage in less enlightened times.

Restoration of the Southern Stratford was undertaken under the aegis of the National Trust. But with completion of the Upper Avon scheme and creation of the Avon Ring, traffic levels increased dramatically, and the body more normally associated with the preservation and upkeep of country houses, found its slim resources stretched by the backlog of maintenance on the canal. In 1977 the National Trust expressed the wish to transfer responsibility for the upkeep of the Southern Stratford to another body, but more than a decade of indecision was to pass before British Waterways assumed control of the canal. It seemed the only sensible solution, particularly as they already were in control of the northern section of the canal between Kingswood and King's Norton. Transfer of ownership was completed in May, 1988 along with a 'dowry' of £1½ million to be spent on maintenance over a period of five years and the small complement of full-time staff who had worked on the canal under the National Trust. One immediate and obvious benefit to boaters following the take-over, was the elimination of the National Trust licence hitherto required for passage along the Southern Stratford.

**Navigation Authority**
British Waterways
Canal Lane
Hatton,
Warwick
CV35 7JL
Tel: Warwick (0926) 492192

**Maximum Dimensions**
Length: 70ft; Width: 7ft; Height; 6ft; Depth: 2½ft.

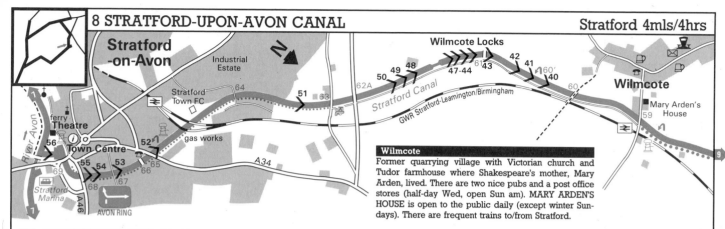

**Wilmcote**

Former quarrying village with Victorian church and Tudor farmhouse where Shakespeare's mother, Mary Arden, lived. There are two nice pubs and a post office stores (half-day Wed, open Sun am). MARY ARDEN'S HOUSE is open to the public daily (except winter Sundays). There are frequent trains to/from Stratford.

LITTLE EVIDENCE SURVIVES of former commercial activity at Stratford Canal Basin. Bordered by the flower beds and park benches of Bancroft Gardens, the basin has the appearence of some municipal ornamental pond. River access is obvious to even the least inquisitive tourist, but egress beneath bridge 69 less so, and because the Stratford Canal curves so unobtrusively around the eastern outskirts of the town, the average visitor is unaware of its existence at all. But once there were *two* basins and the scene was a hive of activity. Timber wharves and tanneries stood alongside the canal and cargoes were transhipped between boats and the wagons of the Stratford & Moreton Horse Tramway. The canal reached here in 1816. Forty years later it was acquired by a constituent of the Great Western Railway. Predictably trade was stifled. The last working boat reached the town in 1920. The rest is history and you will have read about it on the previous page.

In making its exit from (and entrance into) the town, the Stratford Canal negotiates a quartet of locks. To those more familiar with Stratford's gilded thoroughfares, the environs come as something of a surprise; it's like parents discovering a character flaw in a cherished offspring. Gasometers, a canning factory, railway sidings and a football stadium seem at odds with previously held mental images of Shakespeareland. But disillusion is ephemeral, by the time bridge 63 is reached, and the neighbouring, shortlived spa, the town's periphery is all but left behind and the Wilmcote flight of eleven locks lies ahead.

Like Caesar's Gaul and strawberry cheesecake, WILMCOTE LOCKS are divided into three distinct parts; two outer threes and a middle five. In truth they are unexceptional, lacking any particular character of their own. Neither are they much fun to walk beside. For the convenience of maintenance the towpath has been widened and surfaced with an especially painful form of granite chippings. Stout boots, as they say in all good walking guides, are recommended.

BRIDGE 59 was the straw which almost broke the camel's back. Its deterioration caused the local authority to seek permission to abandon the canal back in 1958, so that they could legally replace the bridge by diverting the roadway across the bed of the canal. Apparently evidence as to the canal's use hinged on the purchase of a solitary toll ticket for a canoe the previous year! The only *real* function that the canal performed at the time was to supply water to the engine sheds at Stratford railway station for the cleaning and service of steam engines . Useful moorings have been provided by the local canal society just north of the bridge. South of it you should proceed cautiously for the canal narrows considerably. The quarrying of stone and the burning of lime were two local activities which provided traffic for the canal in earlier years. The abutments of a former tramway bridge recall this activity.

**O**DD LOCK separates two lengthy and predominently remote pounds between the locks at Wilmcote and Preston Bagot. But interest barely falters, because there are two highly characterful aqueducts to be encountered.

EDSTONE AQUEDUCT – sometimes known as Bearley – is undoubtedly the Stratford Canal's most dramatic engineering feature. It consists of an iron trough resting on thirteen tapering brick piers. At 28 feet high and 754 feet long, it seems modest enough, but in the context of the gentle rolling landscape, its sudden appearence has the majesty and startling effect of the renowned Pontcysyllte Aqueduct on the Llangollen Canal. The 'sunken' towpath offers walkers a strange, fish-eye lens view of passing boats. The aqueduct spans a by-road, a tributary of the River Alne, and the twin tracks of the Birmingham & North Warwickshire Railway. Rickety old diesel units rumble under the canal on their way past the isolated signal box at Bearley Junction and down into Stratford.

WOOTTON WAWEN AQUEDUCT is a much more modest affair which fights a running battle with the juggernauts on the A34. On several occasions it has borne the brunt of high-sided vehicles whose drivers grasp of measurements lacked finesse. Nevertheless, it has stood its ground since 1813 and should be good for a few years yet, Ministry of Transport permitting. A hiatus in construction of canal meant that it terminated temporarily at Wootton Wawen for a couple of years, and a sizeable wharf was provided here in the interim. Over a hundred and fifty years later it is used by the only hire boat company operating on the whole of the Stratford Canal.

## Wootton Wawen

A potentially beautiful village spoilt by being on the busy A34 trunk road. Nevertheless, there are some interesting buildings worth taking the trouble to see. The first reached from the canal is a former paper mill, tastefully converted for residential use. This is followed by a graceful bridge over the River Alne which passes over a weir in the grounds of Wootton Hall, a 17th century mansion which once belonged to Mrs Fitzherbert, a mistress of George IV. Next comes the parish church of St Peter; it dates back to Saxon times and is generally considered one of Warwickshire's finest. Access from the canal is best achieved along the lanes from bridges 53 and 54, but there is a surreptitious short cut curving beneath the aqueduct from its southern abutment.

### Boating Facilities

ANGLO-WELSH WATERWAY HOLIDAYS – head office at: The Basin, Market Harborough LE16 7BJ. Tel: (0858) 66910. 2 to 10 berth hire craft. Pumpout, diesel, gas, Elsan & rubbish disposal, repairs, moorings, water and boatbuilding.. Boatyard telephone: Henley-in-Arden (05642) 3427.

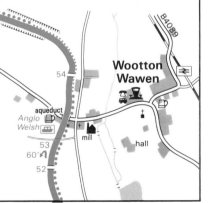

## Eating & Drinking

THE NAVIGATION – canalside at aqueduct. Whitbread, bar and restaurant meals.
OLDE BULLS HEAD – village centre. M&B bar and restaurant meals.

## Shopping

General stores on A34, open daily.

## Public Transport

BUSES – Midland Red South to/from Birmingham & Stratford. Tel: Rugby (0788) 535555.
TRAINS – hourly service to/from Stratford and Birmingham. Tel: 021-200 2601.
*The pretty town of Henley-in-Arden is only 5 miles away (in the Birmingham direction) by bus or train.*

**D**ELICATE SPLIT CANTILEVER BRIDGES and barrel-roofed cottages are two ingredients which lend particular charm to the middle section of the Stratford upon Avon Canal. Actually, they only serve to 'gild the lily', because this length of canal is especially lovely in any case. Between Wootton Wawen and Kingswood the Stratford Canal loses itself in the last vestiges of the old Forest of Arden.

From Preston Bagot to Lowsonford the canal winds its lonely way across Yarningale Common. Yarningale Aqueduct is the baby of the family. The original barrel-roof cottages by locks 34 and 37 have been incorporated in modern extensions. One might have wished they had been left alone, but at least those by locks 28 and 31 remain unspoilt. At the former you can buy hand-painted canal ware; the latter is still in the ownership of the National Trust. Incidentally, the unusual design of these cottages is said to have been brought about by the use of the same wooden frames used in the construction of the brick road bridges which span the canal.

The abutments of a former railway bridge frame the canal near Lowsonford. The bridge carried a branchline to Henley-in-Arden, closed when the route was made obsolete by opening of the North Warwickshire Railway. Legend has it that the track was despatched to The Front during the Great War but ended up at the bottom of the English Channel. It seems unlikely that the new motorway will be as shortlived as the railway. We came down here on a research trip just before it was due to open, wondering if birdsong would ever be heard in this valley again.

The novelist, Temple Thurston, wrote lovingly of this part of the Stratford Canal in his somewhat romanticised waterway classic "The Flower of Gloucester". In 1910 he had hired a narrowboat, a horse and a boatman, and had set off from Oxford in search of copy for the sort of travel book in vogue at the time. On the advice of his boatman – who rejoiced in the name of 'Eynsham Harry' – they had turned off the Warwick & Birmingham at Kingswood Junction to discover the rural delights of the Straford Canal. It was already little used, and Temple Thurston described it as being "right out of the track of the world". He climbed the hillside to a farm at Yarningale for fresh milk, and Eynsham Harry bought beer from the wife of a lock-keeper. Reading his book as you travel along the canal today leads, inevitably, to melancholy comparisons.

**Eating & Drinking**

CRAB MILL – adjacent bridge 48. Comfortable country pub which used to be a cider mill, hence the name. Meals usually available, families welcome. Good range of ale including: Marstons and Wadworth.

HAVEN TEA ROOMS – canalside by lock 38. Informal and inexpensive cafe for lunches and teas.

FLEUR DE LYS – canalside bridge 41. Well appointed country inn dating from 14th century. Customer moorings. Bar and restaurant meals. Whitbread.

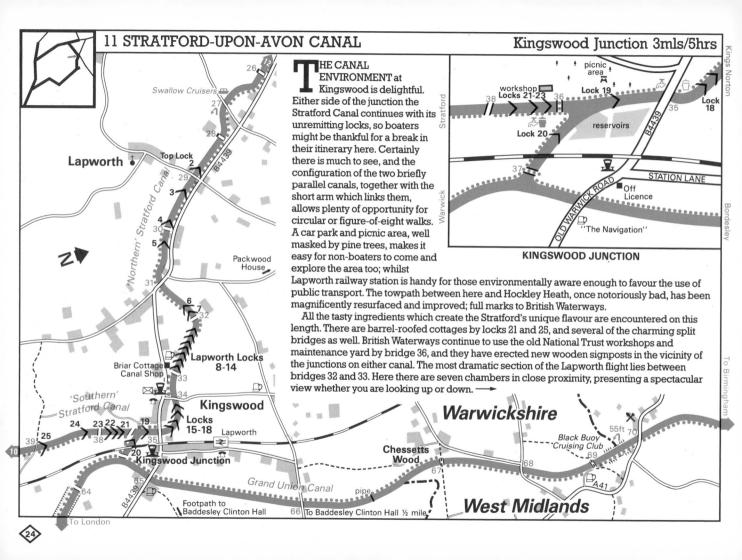

**KINGSWOOD JUNCTION**

THE CANAL ENVIRONMENT at Kingswood is delightful. Either side of the junction the Stratford Canal continues with its unremitting locks, so boaters might be thankful for a break in their itinerary here. Certainly there is much to see, and the configuration of the two briefly parallel canals, together with the short arm which links them, allows plenty of opportunity for circular or figure-of-eight walks. A car park and picnic area, well masked by pine trees, makes it easy for non-boaters to come and explore the area too; whilst Lapworth railway station is handy for those environmentally aware enough to favour the use of public transport. The towpath between here and Hockley Heath, once notoriously bad, has been magnificently resurfaced and improved; full marks to British Waterways.

All the tasty ingredients which create the Stratford's unique flavour are encountered on this length. There are barrel-roofed cottages by locks 21 and 25, and several of the charming split bridges as well. British Waterways continue to use the old National Trust workshops and maintenance yard by bridge 36, and they have erected new wooden signposts in the vicinity of the junctions on either canal. The most dramatic section of the Lapworth flight lies between bridges 32 and 33. Here there are seven chambers in close proximity, presenting a spectacular view whether you are looking up or down. →

Bridges 26 and 28 are lifting structures, the former of Llangollen pattern, the latter reminiscent of those found on the Oxford Canal; though here operation is by way of a winch for which you will need a windlass. Bridge 27 was the temporary southern terminus of the canal between 1796 and 1800. It actually took 22 years to build the 25 mile long canal between King's Norton and Stratford. The summit cost as much to make as the budget for the whole canal. The engineer was Josiah Clowes, a somewhat shadowy figure associated with a number of late 18th century waterway structures; notably Sapperton and Dudley tunnels. In any case, he died (possibly of boredom) before Hockley Heath was reached, and two other engineers were involved in the canal's dilatory progress down to the Avon.

### Eating & Drinking

THE NAVIGATION – canalside bridge 65 (Grand Union). M&B, bar food, garden & payphone. Pleasantly unspoilt, popular with boaters.

THE BOOT – adjacent bridge 33. Flowers ales, good bar food, convivial atmosphere.

### Shopping

General store with newspapers, and off licence, east of bridge 35. Post office stores and butcher by bridge 34. BRIAR COTTAGE is a delightful canal shop. Fresh dairy produce is available here together with a useful selection of groceries and frozen foods. Delicious home made cakes usually on sale too. Also lots of nice crafts, gifts and canal souvenirs.

### Things to Do

PACKWOOD HOUSE – access from bridge 31. Tudor house with celebrated formal yew garden said to represent the Sermon on the Mount. Inside are panelled rooms containing a fine selection of tapestries, textiles and furniture. Open Wed-Sun afternoons mid-March to end October. Admission charge. Picnic area and National Trust shop. Tel: Lapworth (05643) 2024. Also nearby, BADDESLEY CLINTON HALL.

### Public Transport

TRAINS – local trains to/from Birmingham, Warwick & Leamington from *Lapworth* station. Tel: 021-200 2601.

### Boating Facilities

SWALLOW CRUISERS – Wharf Lane, Hockley Heath. Tel: Lapworth (05643) 3442. Water, diesel, Calor gas, moorings, slipway, day boat hire, boat sales and brokerage, Honda outboards, shop with off licence and provisions.

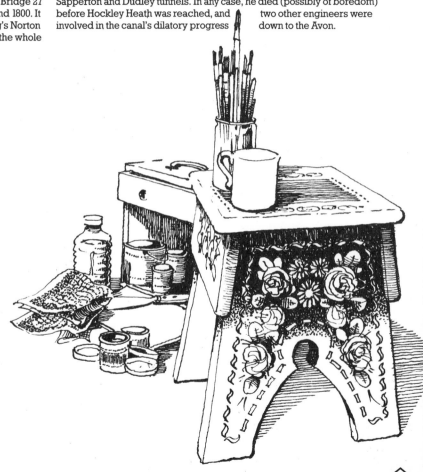

**N**ORTH OF HOCKLEY HEATH the canal assumes a mantle of trees which border much of the summit section. Oak, alder, hazel and willow predominate, creating a soothing, sylvan quality which is apt to become somewhat soporific after a while. Such lush vegetation has encroached upon the towpath in most places, rendering the North Stratford a canal not easily walked. When you do catch glimpses of the surrounding countryside, it reminds you of the Home Counties, exuding an air of affluence epitomised by large detached houses, and horsey young ladies, trotting down dappled lanes on dappled steeds.

The winding-hole by bridge 22 marks the site of a wharf once linked by tramway to the limestone quarries of Tanworth-in-Arden. Originally a branch canal had been planned to cater for this traffic. For a mile or two the canal forms the county boundary between Warwickshire and the dolefully named West Midlands.

At Earlswood an embankment carries the canal over Spring Brook and a feeder enters the canal from a trio of reservoirs which lie to the south-west. These Earlswood Reservoirs are a popular ammenity, attracting ramblers, anglers and bird-watchers. Even if you have more enthusiasm for machinery than wildlife, the reservoirs are still worth visiting, to see the old

engine house on Lady Lane, to which narrowboats carried coal up the feeder until 1936.

**Summary of Facilities**

A good complement of pubs add needed diversion to the sylvan monotony of the North Stratford. Two canalside inns on this section are: THE WHARF TAVERN, bridge 25, a popular 'Chef & Brewer' house with Ruddles and Websters on tap, an excellent carvery and framed photographs on the walls of narrowboats by Mike Webb. Children are welcome to accompany parents if on their best behaviour! Alternatively try the BLUE BELL CIDER HOUSE by bridge 19, where they do a variety of draught beers and ciders, bar meals are usually available here and there's a pleasant garden and play area.

Hockley Heath has a good range of shops best approached from bridge 25. Down the lane from bridge 20 stands WEDGE'S BAKERY whose cream cakes are good for morale.

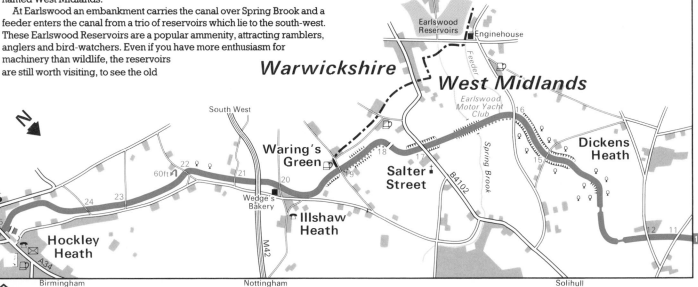

**A**LTHOUGH THE MAP emphasises how built-up these south-western suburbs of Birmingham are, the canal seems oblivious to the proximity of so many houses and people, retaining an aloof quality, like a recluse in a crowd. Progress falters as you are forced to slow past boats moored at the bottom of just about every other garden. Paradoxically, passing boaters have little chance of mooring because of the badly eroded towpath. Only to the north of bridge 8, by the water point at bridge 5, and at Lyons boatyard is casual mooring feasible.

Brandwood Tunnel comes as a welcome respite from the claustrophobia of the wooded cuttings. No towpath was provided, so horses were led over the top while boats were worked through by the simple expedient of boatmen pulling on a handrail set into the tunnel lining. The northern portal carried a carving of the company's seal – including Shakespeare's profile – but this is pretty well eroded now. Between the tunnel and King's Norton Junction is Lifford Lane bridge, a *cause celebre* in the embryonic days of the Inland Waterways Association. It used to be a lifting bridge and, during the war the Great Western Railway, who owned the canal at that time, clamped down the platform following damage by a lorry. Commercial traffic had ceased using the canal, but the IWA maintained that a right of navigation still applied. The GWR claimed that they would be only too happy to jack up the bridge to permit boats to pass beneath it, little realising that the IWA intended to organise as many boat passages as would be necessary to have the bridge properly repaired. Several campaign cruises along the North Stratford ensued, but it was not until Nationalisation that the present swing bridge was installed.

The final (or first) surprise that the North Stratford has to offer, is an unusual 'guillotine' stop lock. The vertically lifting wooden gates, mounted in iron frames and balanced by chains and counterweights, could work either way, irrespective of which canal had the higher water level. Since 1948, when the Stratford-on-Avon and Worcester & Birmingham canals were Nationalised, the guillotines have remained permanently raised.

### Eating & Drinking

THE DRAW BRIDGE – canalside bridge 8. Davenports, bar meals, garden.

THE HORSESHOES – canalside bridge 3. M&B, bar meals, garden.

### Shopping

Good range of suburban shops, banks etc at Warstock; access from bridge 5.

### Boating Facilities

FRANK LYONS – Lime Kiln Lane, Warstock, Birmingham B14 4SX. 021-474 4977. Diesel, Calor gas, pumpout, water, Elsan disposal, toilets, showers, moorings, boat & engine sales, repairs & servicing, lifting up to 7 tons. Also: RAY'S PLACE for gifts, brassware and chandlery. Open daily.

King's Norton Junction

Guillotine Stop Lock

Chemical Works

Brandwood Tunnel 322m

Whitlocks End

60 ft

River Cole

Major's Green

Warstock

Shirley

Lyons

GW North Warks Line

WORCESTER & BIRMINGHAM CANAL

Tardebigge Locks.

**T**HE WORCESTER & BIRMINGHAM is not a charismatic canal. You can't imagine anyone falling in love with it the way they do its near neighbour, the Staffs & Worcs. But in its thirty miles it boasts five tunnels, the longest flight of locks in the country, and by far the prettiest way of leaving (or reaching) Birmingham.

It took longer to complete than the Stratford Canal – and that's saying something – being 24 years in the making. The men who promoted it, wanted a more direct route between Birmingham and the River Severn than the Dudley, Stourbridge and Staffs & Worcs canals could offer. They had delusions of wide-beam grandeur, but though the bridges and tunnels bear evidence of this aspiration, there was just not enough money available to build the great number of locks to the larger gauge. Numerous reservoirs had to be constructed as well, not only to feed the canal, but also to compensate millers on the rivers Rea and Arrow from which the canal drew water. The canal opened throughout from Gas Street to Diglis in 1815. Trade built up slowly but steadily; being boosted by completion of the Gloucester & Sharpness ship canal and by the company's lease of the Lower Avon. But following the opening of the Birmingham & Gloucester Railway in 1841, traffic levels – like the canal itself – went downhill, and even after the Sharpness New Docks Company had acquired the canal and tried to resuscitate trade, it never really paid its way. Nowadays, however, the Worcester & Birmingham Canal is an important link in the inland waterways network, being part and parcel of the popular Avon and Stourport 'rings', and in the cruising season Tardebigge locks are busier than they ever were in the canal's cargo carrying days.

**Navigation Authority**
British Waterways
Canal Office
New Wharf
Tardebigge
Bromsgrove
Worcs. B60 1NF
Tel: Bromsgrove (0527) 72572

**Maximum Dimensions**
Length 70ft, beam 7ft, height 6ft, draught 2½ft.

Healings grain barges, Tewkesbury

Cropthorne Mill, Lower Avon Navigation

Narrowboats near Luddington, Upper Avon Navigation

The ferry, Stratford-on-Avon

Barrel-roofed cottage and split bridge on the Stratford Canal

Tardebigge New Wharf, Worcester & Birmingham Canal

Holt Lock, River Severn

The National Waterways Museum, Gloucester Docks

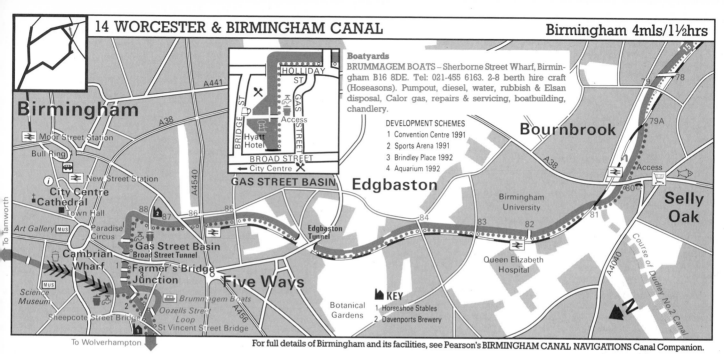

**Birmingham**

Moor Street Station

Bull Ring

New Street Station

City Centre Cathedral

Town Hall

Art Gallery

Paradise Circus

Cambrian Wharf

Gas Street Basin
Broad Street Tunnel

Farmer's Bridge Junction

Science Museum

Sheepcote Street Bridge

Oozells Street Loop

St Vincent Street Bridge

Brummagem Boats

**Five Ways**

To Tamworth

To Wolverhampton

HOLLIDAY ST

BRIDGE ST

GAS STREET

Access

Hyatt Hotel

BROAD STREET

← City Centre

**GAS STREET BASIN**

**Edgbaston**

Edgbaston Tunnel

**Boatyards**

BRUMMAGEM BOATS – Sherborne Street Wharf, Birmingham B16 8DE. Tel: 021-455 6163. 2-8 berth hire craft (Hoseasons). Pumpout, diesel, water, rubbish & Elsan disposal, Calor gas, repairs & servicing, boatbuilding, chandlery.

DEVELOPMENT SCHEMES
1  Convention Centre 1991
2  Sports Arena 1991
3  Brindley Place 1992
4  Aquarium 1992

**Bournbrook**

**Selly Oak**

Birmingham University

Queen Elizabeth Hospital

Botanical Gardens

Course of Dudley No.2 Canal

Access

**KEY**
1  Horseshoe Stables
2  Davenports Brewery

For full details of Birmingham and its facilities, see Pearson's BIRMINGHAM CANAL NAVIGATIONS Canal Companion.

T HE WORCESTER & BIRMINGHAM CANAL forms a junction with the Birmingham Canal Navigations in the celebrated surroundings of Gas Street Basin. Here was the infamous 'Worcester Bar', a seven foot divide across which through goods had to be laboriously transhipped for several years following completion of the Worcester & Birmingham, because the Birmingham Canal feared that its precious water supply would disappear down into the River Severn. Ten years of inconvenience passed before the BCN permitted the barrier to be replaced by a stop lock; its site remains evident to this day. Gas Street Basin itself, and the magical world of the BCN beyond, are described fully in "Pearson's Birmingham Canal Navigations Canal Companion".

South-westwards from Gas Street, the Worcester & Birmingham Canal crosses an impressive but little known aqueduct supported on ornamental cast iron columns (best appreciated from street level) and then turns sharply, shaking off the city and delving into Edgbaston's well-heeled and sylvan suburbs. It was this cloistered and aboreous approach of the canal into the city which prompted Robert Aickman to express that 'Canals stretch green fingers into towns', and certainly it is hard to accept that this seemingly remote canal lies just a stone's throw from the pulsating heart of the Second City. Only at Selly Oak is the spell briefly broken by the appearence of factory walls. Otherwise the canal traveller has nothing else to do but watch for squirrels in the overhanging trees and wave regally at the passing trains.

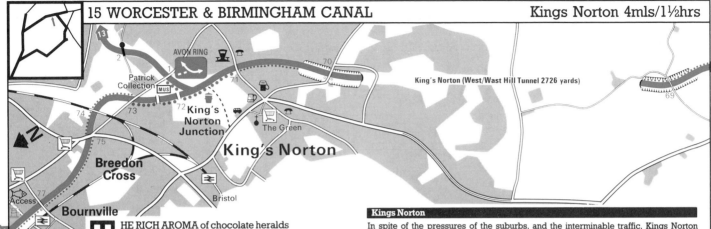

THE RICH AROMA of chocolate heralds BOURNVILLE and Cadbury's famous factory. They have opened a visitor centre here and, unlike Charlie Bucket, you don't need a golden ticket to get in!

Another 'Chocolate Charlie' – as well known in canal circles as Roald Dahl's character is in children's literature – was Charlie Atkins senior, one of the last captains to work boats between Bournville and Cadbury's canalside plant at Knighton on the Shropshire Union Canal. Cadbury had a history of waterway activities. They operated their own fleet of narrowboats, the distinctive livery of which inspired Brian Collings' front cover design. Bourneville once boasted extensive wharves and warehouses, located on the eastern bank of the canal on a site now occupied by pleasant modern housing.

At KING'S NORTON JUNCTION the Patrick Collection provides another magnet for visitors. Here, in premises which once housed a paper mill is a unique collection of motor cars. The junction itself is presided over by a handsome canal house. Pleasant moorings are available between bridges 71 and 72, with an outlook onto a large expanse of playing fields.

King's Norton Tunnel is the longest on the Worcester & Birmingham Canal. It takes around half an hour to boat through it and, although appearances can be deceptive, there *is* room to pass oncoming craft inside its gloomy depths.

In spite of the pressures of the suburbs, and the interminable traffic, Kings Norton retains a fragile village feel, enhanced by the survival of the (possibly pre-Norman) green. 'The Mop', a former hiring fair with its origins steeped in the Middle Ages, is still held on the first Monday in October. Enthusiasts of church architecture will want to visit the impressive 14th century church. Tucked away in a shadowy corner of the graveyard lurks the half-timbered old Grammar School. Grouped about the village green are numerous useful shops (including chemist, launderette, delicatessen, off licence and Lloyd's Bank) a Chinese take away and an Indian restaurant. Frequent buses head for Birmingham, as do trains from the station ½ mile north along the A441.

### Things to Do

CADBURY WORLD – Linden Road, Bournville, Birmingham B30 2LU. Tel: 021-433 4334. Access from offside moorings north of bridge 77. Pass under canal and railway, Linden Road is first turn on right. Open daily, admission charge. Publicised as 'The Chocolate Experience', Cadbury's new visitor centre celebrates the history of chcolate, highlighting its origins in Central America, the development of the family business, the company's long success with advertising and publicity, and – of special interest to canal fans – the transport of raw materials and finished products. Modern day production methods are exhibited too and, naturally, there's a gift shop dispensing souvenirs and a special Cadbury World assortment box.

THE PATRICK COLLECTION – 180 Lifford Lang, King's Norton. Tel: 021-459 9111. Visitor moorings adjacent bridge 72. Open daily Easter to October. Admission charge. Exciting 'museum' of motor and racing cars imaginatively displayed in two exhibition halls along with authentic period settings. Restaurant cafeteria,, landscaped grounds, souvenir shop and children's play area.

THE CANAL WORMS its secluded way around the hillside above Alvechurch. There are panoramic views eastwards over windmill-topped Weatheroak Hill, crossed by the Roman's Ryknild Street which you'll meet again at Bidford-on-Avon if you are doing the whole of the Avon Ring.

A feeder comes in from the Upper Bittell reservoir beside an isolated canal employee's cottage near bridge 66. The Lower reservoir, rich in wildfowl, lies alongside the canal and has a gorgeous wooded backdrop crowned by the Lickey Hills. Only the upper reservoir feeds the canal. The lower was provided by the canal company to compensate millers in the vicinity whose water supplies from the river Arrow had been affected by construction of the canal. In 1985 a short section of the canal was re-routed to accommodate construction of the M42 motorway. The old course of the canal disappears beneath bridge 64A.

The single track railway to Redditch – a branch which leaves the main line at nearby Barnt Green – somehow survived Beeching and is now a flourishing commuter link with prospects of being electrified as part of the Birmingham 'Cross-City' line. Alvechurch station retains all the allure of a country halt, and we can recommend the pretty ride down the valley of the Arrow to the terminus. Originally the line went through to Evesham; ring travellers will see its dismantled course in the vicinity of Offenham. The railway junction at Barnt Green lies near the top of the famous Lickey Incline; at 1 in 37, the steepest main line gradient on British Rail. It emphasises the steepness of the climb out of the Severn Valley on to the Birmingham escarpment, and is the railway equivalent of the great Tardebigge flight of locks.

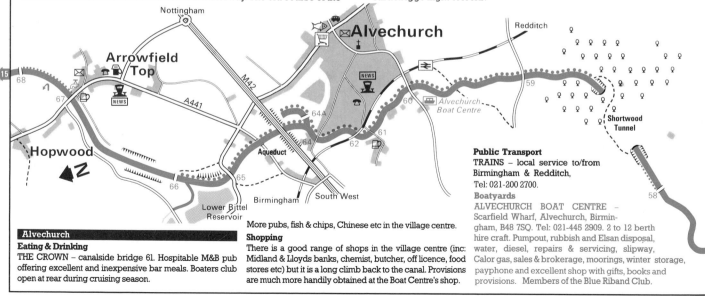

## Alvechurch
### Eating & Drinking
THE CROWN – canalside bridge 61. Hospitable M&B pub offering excellent and inexpensive bar meals. Boaters club open at rear during cruising season.

More pubs, fish & chips, Chinese etc in the village centre.

### Shopping
There is a good range of shops in the village centre (inc: Midland & Lloyds banks, chemist, butcher, off licence, food stores etc) but it is a long climb back to the canal. Provisions are much more handily obtained at the Boat Centre's shop.

### Public Transport
TRAINS – local service to/from Birmingham & Redditch,
Tel: 021-200 2700.
### Boatyards
ALVECHURCH BOAT CENTRE – Scarfield Wharf, Alvechurch, Birmingham, B48 7SQ. Tel: 021-445 2909. 2 to 12 berth hire craft. Pumpout, rubbish and Elsan disposal, water, diesel, repairs & servicing, slipway, Calor gas, sales & brokerage, moorings, winter storage, payphone and excellent shop with gifts, books and provisions. Members of the Blue Riband Club.

TARDEBIGGE LOCKS represents a boater's Rite of Passage. Once you have tackled this flight which, taken with the neighbouring six at Stoke, amount to thirty-six locks in four miles, other groups of locks seem small beer. The Thirty chambers of the Tardebigge flight raise the canal 217 feet; the top lock being, at 14 feet, one of the deepest narrowbeam locks on the system. Happily the flight is in good condition, and the lock-wheeler has time to appreciate the stunning views offered towards the Malvern Hills.

Tardebigge itself holds a special place in the story of the inland waterways movement. It was here that Robert Aickman made his way from Bromsgrove station to meet Tom and Angela Rolt aboard their narrowboat home, *Cressy*, which had been moored above the top lock throughout the war. As a direct result of their meeting the Inland Waterways Association was formed. A plinth adjacent to the lock tells the story, though there is some debate as to whether their first meeting took place in 1946, as stated, or in the previous year.

Tom Rolt painted vivid pictures of the canal at Tardebigge in two of his books: "Worcestershire", published by Robert Hale in 1949, and "Landscape with Canals", by Allen Lane in 1977. Another portrait of the canalside community appeared in "Lock Keeper's Daughter" by Pat Warner (Shepperton Swan 1986). All three books give the impression of an unchanging pattern of life centred on the canal and its trade, peopled by a cast of tug captains, reservoir keepers and lockgate makers. From the vantage point of the Nineties it seems an idyllic way of life, but there is still a welcome timelessness about Tardebigge which makes visiting here a rewarding experience.

## Tardebigge

There are no shops or pubs within easy walking reach of the canal. The old Engine House by bridge 55 – once employed in back-pumping water from the reservoir to the summit – is now a restaurant and night-club; telephone Bromsgrove 35238 for reservations. Midland Red West buses operate hourly Mon-Sat from stops adjacent to the southern portal of the tunnel to Bromsgrove and Redditch.

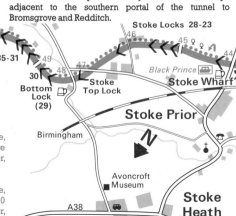

*(Map: Worcester & Birmingham Canal, Tardebigge)*

Redditch — Tardebigge — Top Lock (58) — Tardebigge Tunnel (530 metres) — Aickman/Rolt plaque — BW Section Office — Kidderminster — A448 — Dartline — 57 — 56 — 55 — 57-50 — Engine House — Tardebigge Reservoir — 54 — Tardebigge Locks 58-29 — 49-45 — 52 — 51 — 44-41 — 40-36 — Bromsgrove 1½ miles — 50 — 35-31 — 49 — 48 — 47 — 30 — Bottom Lock (29) — Stoke Top Lock — Stoke Locks 28-23 — 46 — 45 — 44 — Black Prince — Stoke Wharf — Stoke Prior — Birmingham — N — Avoncroft Museum — A38 — Stoke Heath — Bristol

## Stoke Prior

Canalside pubs at bridges 44 and 48; THE NAVIGATION and QUEEN'S HEAD respectively. The latter is a particularly popular port of call for boaters, being highly regarded for its bar and restaurant meals. JAN'S KITCHEN (bridge 44) is open daily throughout the summer months for breakfasts and lunches. Evening meals can be arranged by appointment on Bromsgrove 79726. Less than a mile west of bridge 48 lies AVONCROFT, an outdoor museum of buildings – one of its exhibits, a weatherboarded windmill, can be glimpsed from the canal. Its open daily throughout the summer and on selected days during the winter. Tel: Bromsgrove (0527) 31886 for further details.

**Boating Facilities**

DARTLINE – Old Wharf, Tardebigge, Bromsgrove, Worcs. Tel: Bromsgrove (0527) 73898. 2 to 12 berth hire craft. Pumpout, diesel, Elsan & rubbish disposal, water, moorings, gift shop and payphone.

BLACK PRINCE HOLIDAYS – Stoke Prior, Bromsgrove, Worcs B60 4LA. Tel: Bromsgrove (0527) 575115. 2 to 10 berth hire craft. Pumpout, Elsan & rubbih disposal, water, diesel, gas, moorings.

NOWADAYS, BRITAIN'S SALT industry is largely confined to Cheshire but, as the name Droitwich suggests, this part of Worcestershire was once a centre of salt making too. The salt obsessed Romans built a special road between Droitwich and Alcester to carry this valuable commodity. Its course crosses the canal at Hanbury Wharf. Several thousand years later the Worcester & Birmingham built the short Droitwich Junction Canal from here down into the town to carry the same cargo. Barely two miles long, it included seven locks and passed briefly into the River Salwarpe before meeting the previously established Droitwich Canal at Vines Park near the centre of the town. Both of the Droitwich canals were derelict before the Second World War, but in recent years they have undergone varying degrees of restoration. At Hanbury Wharf the top pound of the Junction Canal has been re-watered and is in use as private moorings. A trip boat operates out of Droitwich along the summit of the wide beam Droitwich Canal.

At the end of the 18th century, John Corbett, the son of a local boatman, discovered large deposits of brine beneath the surface at Stoke Prior and subsequently built a salt works on the site. It made his fortune. He married a French woman and built her a replica chateau in the nearby Worcestershire countryside, and he was in the forefront of the development of Droitwich as a spa town. Unfortunately, Droitwich's salt trade was killed off by the machinations of 'The Salt Union', a trade cartel which backfired on many of its members. The salt works at Stoke has long been closed.

Railway and canal join forces again beside the Astwood flight, and drift lazily through pleasant farmland. From the Bottom Lock (No.17) a footpath leads across the fields to Hanbury Hall, a National Trust property open to the public. Westwards there are views towards the Abberley Hills and, nearer by, the tall radio masts at Wychbold, a transmitting station dating from the early Thirties whose call sign was 'Droitwich Calling'. The masts may be demolished in the near future.

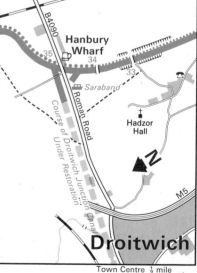

## Hanbury Wharf

**Eating & Drinking**

EAGLE & SUN – adjacent bridge 35. M&B beers and bar meals.

**Boatyard**

SARABAND – Hanbury Wharf, Droitwich, Worcs WR9 7DU. Tel: Droitwich (0905) 771018. Diesel, water, Calor gas, repairs & servicing, boatbuilding, sales & brokerage, slipway, payphone, chandlery and groceries.

## Stoke Works

Prosaically named after the enormous salt works, now largely demolished and replaced by a high-tech pharmaceutical factory.

**Eating & Drinking**

THE BOWLING GREEN – ¼ mile west of bridge 41. Banks's, food, garden & bowls.

BOAT & RAILWAY – canalside bridge 42. Hanson's, snacks, skittle alley, customer moorings. Further pub, plus fish & chip shop on road through village.

**Shopping**

Small food shop, open Mon–Sat & Sun am.

**Public Transport**

BUSES – Midland Red West to/from Droitwich & Bromsgrove Mon–Sat. Tel: Bromsgrove (0527) 72265. This approximately bi-hourly service passes close to Avoncroft Museum on its way to Bromsgrove.

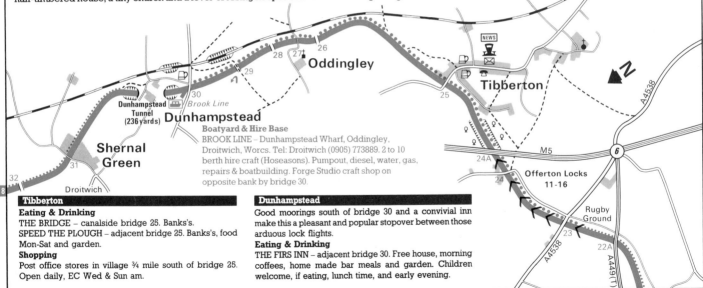

THE CANAL SKIRTS the mellow settlements of Shernal Green, Dunhampstead, Oddingley and Tibberton.

In spite of being sandwiched by the motorway and the railway, the waterway seems remote. High clumps of sedge border the canal, swaying with the passage of each boat and somehow emphasising the loneliness of the landscape. Occasionally a by-road crosses the canal, wandering eastwards into an empty tract of countryside which was once part of the Royal Forest of Feckenham. Incidentally, the River Avon is only a dozen miles away from here as the crow flies.

At 236 yards, Dunhampstead tunnel is the shortest of the five on this canal. Towpath walkers must leave or rejoin the canal at bridge 30 and use the adjacent country road, because the towpath no longer extends to the southern portal of the tunnel. Oddingley consists of little more than an ancient half-timbered house, a tiny church and a level-crossing keeper's house and

cabin. Tibberton, on the other hand, is a long straggling village of mostly modern housing. Offerton Locks lie in a pretty setting, if you can mentally ignore the electricity pylons and the motorway. The big farm by bridge 24 has some gorgeous weather-boarded barns.

Two aspects of the Worcester & Birmingham Canal's working practice were remarkable. Boats kept left when passing each other and pairs of donkeys were widely used in place of horses to haul the boats. Apparently the animals worked well together as long as they 'knew' each other, but the introduction of a new donkey could cause considerable ructions. One of the last traders on the canal was Charles Ballinger of Gloucester. He was still using horse-drawn boats as late as 1954, carrying coal from the Cannock area to Townsend's mill at Diglis. Occasionally he would have an 'uphill' cargo too: matches from Gloucester to Birmingham, or flour from Worcester to Tipton; but by the beginning of the Sixties trade had deserted the canal.

**Dunhampstead Tunnel (236 yards)**

**Dunhampstead**

**Boatyard & Hire Base**
BROOK LINE – Dunhampstead Wharf, Oddingley, Droitwich, Worcs. Tel: Droitwich (0905) 773889. 2 to 10 berth hire craft (Hoseasons). Pumpout, diesel, water, gas, repairs & boatbuilding. Forge Studio craft shop on opposite bank by bridge 30.

**Shernal Green**

Droitwich

**Oddingley**

**Tibberton**

**Offerton Locks 11-16**

Rugby Ground

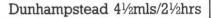

### Tibberton

**Eating & Drinking**
THE BRIDGE – canalside bridge 25. Banks's.
SPEED THE PLOUGH – adjacent bridge 25. Banks's, food Mon-Sat and garden.

**Shopping**
Post office stores in village ¾ mile south of bridge 25. Open daily, EC Wed & Sun am.

### Dunhampstead

Good moorings south of bridge 30 and a convivial inn make this a pleasant and popular stopover between those arduous lock flights.

**Eating & Drinking**
THE FIRS INN – adjacent bridge 30. Free house, morning coffees, home made bar meals and garden. Children welcome, if eating, lunch time, and early evening.

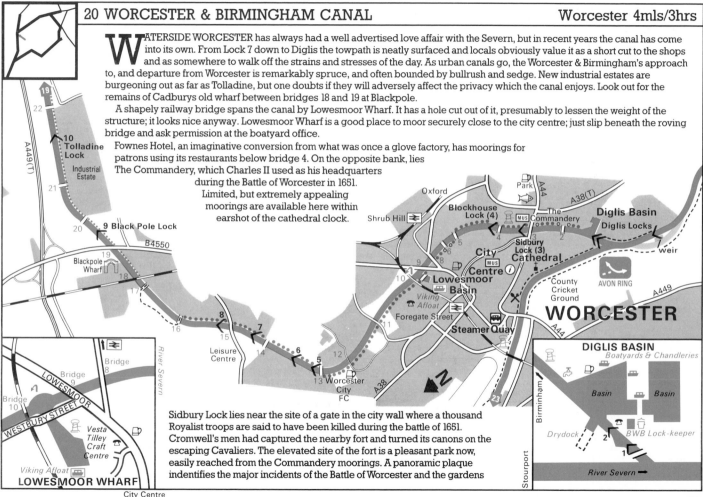

**W**ATERSIDE WORCESTER has always had a well advertised love affair with the Severn, but in recent years the canal has come into its own. From Lock 7 down to Diglis the towpath is neatly surfaced and locals obviously value it as a short cut to the shops and as somewhere to walk off the strains and stresses of the day. As urban canals go, the Worcester & Birmingham's approach to, and departure from Worcester is remarkably spruce, and often bounded by bullrush and sedge. New industrial estates are burgeoning out as far as Tolladine, but one doubts if they will adversely affect the privacy which the canal enjoys. Look out for the remains of Cadburys old wharf between bridges 18 and 19 at Blackpole.

A shapely railway bridge spans the canal by Lowesmoor Wharf. It has a hole cut out of it, presumably to lessen the weight of the structure; it looks nice anyway. Lowesmoor Wharf is a good place to moor securely close to the city centre; just slip beneath the roving bridge and ask permission at the boatyard office.

Fownes Hotel, an imaginative conversion from what was once a glove factory, has moorings for patrons using its restaurants below bridge 4. On the opposite bank, lies The Commandery, which Charles II used as his headquarters during the Battle of Worcester in 1651. Limited, but extremely appealing moorings are available here within earshot of the cathedral clock.

Sidbury Lock lies near the site of a gate in the city wall where a thousand Royalist troops are said to have been killed during the battle of 1651. Cromwell's men had captured the nearby fort and turned its canons on the escaping Cavaliers. The elevated site of the fort is a pleasant park now, easily reached from the Commandery moorings. A panoramic plaque identifies the major incidents of the Battle of Worcester and the gardens

**10 Tolladine Lock**

Industrial Estate

**9 Black Pole Lock**

B4550

Blackpole Wharf

**LOWESMOOR WHARF**

Bridge 9
Bridge 8
Bridge 10
LOWESMOOR
WESTBURY STREET
Vesta Tilley Craft Centre
Viking Afloat
City Centre
River Severn

Oxford
Shrub Hill
Park
The Commandery
Blockhouse Lock (4)
City Centre
Lowesmoor Basin
Viking Afloat
Foregate Street
Sidbury Lock (3)
Cathedral
County Cricket Ground
AVON RING
Steamer Quay
Worcester City FC
Leisure Centre

**WORCESTER**

**Diglis Basin**
Diglis Locks
weir

**DIGLIS BASIN**
Boatyards & Chandleries
Basin
Basin
Drydock
BWB Lock-keeper
River Severn →
Stourport
Tewkesbury
Birmingham

offer a marvellous view over the city.

Further moorings are available between bridge 2 and Diglis, and are overlooked by the porcelain factory whose workforce have a distinctly earthy sense of humour. Coal was delivered here by narrowboat until 1961. Part of the pottery works has extended into the former flour mill of Townsend & Co by bridge 2, this was also an important customer of the canal's in working boat days. Diglis Basins were opened early in the 19th century to facilitate transhipment of cargoes between the river and the canal. It would be nice to see the basins full of sailing trows and narrowboats, but any disappointment is soon overtaken by curiosity, for these days they are full of boats familiar with the slap of saltwater beneath

their hulls. So Diglis is a wonderful place to go wandering around, amidst the smell of paint and tar and the noise of wood being sawn and metal bent. Many of the boats are residential and bear ports of origin on their transoms like Bristol, Southampton and London, engendering a real sense of travel and distance and romance.

Two broad locks separate the basins from the river. They are closed at night, re-opening around eight in the morning when the lock-keeper comes on duty. In most cases he doesn't get involved in operating them, but it's good to know he's around should you need his help or advice. Entering or leaving the river can pose problems, especially if the current is fast, so getting your crew on or off for the locks needs careful consideration.

## Worcester

Descending from Birmingham to Worcester, the West Midlands are subtly left behind, and you will find yourself in streets where the *patois* has a distinctly West Country burr. Royal Worcester suffered more than most at the hands of the developers during the sixties (Ian Nairn, the late architectural writer, was incensed) but much making of amends has been done in recent years to enhance the city's fabric. The Cathedral, gazing tenderly out over the river Severn, belongs – along with Gloucester and Hereford - to a gorgeous golden triangle of ecclesiastical materpieces which share, each in turn over three years, Europe's oldest music festival, 'The Three Choirs'. Worcester's is a rich and varied history: the 'faithful city' of the Civil War from which Charles II escaped following the final defeat of the Cavaliers; the home, for much of his life, of one of the great English composers, Sir Edward Elgar; the manufacturing place of Royal Worcester Porcelain and Lea & Perrins Sauce; and the site of one of the country's loveliest cricketing venues, Worcestershire's New Road ground. So, there must surely be something here to capture the imagination of any waterborne visitor to the city; even if you simply want to perambulate the commendably signposted streets and pathways.

### Eating & Drinking

JOLLY ROGER BREWERY & TAP – 50 Lowesmoor. Easy access from bridge 8 or Lowesmoor Basin. They brew their own imaginative range of beers on the premises, the mash tuns being plainly visible from the bar. Of particular interest to boaters must be 'Severn Bore Special', a

distinctively dark, strong beer. Lunches, children welcome.
LITTLE SAUCE FACTORY – London Road, Little Pub Co. establishment celebrating Worcester's saucy past. Excellent food and eccentric atmosphere as usual. Located just uphill from McTaffish by Sidbury Lock.
CADENCE CAFE – Foregate Street Station. A station buffet with a difference. You know your sandwiches are fresh because they make them in front of your eyes. Delicious cakes which they try to persuade you to take with a dollop of ice cream. You can 'eat in' or 'take away'. It may have to be the latter, for there is barely room to brandish a Bradshaw amidst the half dozen or so prettily laid tables. Open from 8 in the morning until the 5.44pm departs for Hereford! Also do cycle hire – Can you Tandem? Tel: Worcester (0905) 613501.

### Shopping

Worcester is an excellent city in which to shop. Two recently restored shopping areas are The Hopmarket and Crown Passage. The Shambles, Friar Street and New Street feature numerous fascinating little shops and small businesses. If however, you're committing the cardinal sin of boating through Worcester non-stop, then a number of useful provisions shops (and a first class fish & chip shop – McTaffish's) can be easily reached to the east of bridge 3 adjacent to The Commandery.

### Places to Visit

THE COMMANDERY – canalside Sidbury Lock. Open daily (afternoons only on Sun). Admission charge. Tel: Worcester 355071. Mainly 16th century building housing

displays relating to Worcester's working and waring past. Particular emphasis on Worcester's part in the Civil War.
THE GREYFRIARS – Friar Street. Open Apr-Oct, Wed, Thur & Bank hol Mons, 2-6pm. Admission charge. Tel: Worcester 23571. Medieval timber-framed house with panelled rooms, and interesting furniture owned by the National Trust.
VESTA TILLEY CENTRE – Lowesmoor. Crafts and collectables; pine furniture and dried flowers; refreshments. Tel: Worcester 726506.
DYSON PERRINS MUSEUM – Severn Street. Open Mon-Sat, 9.00-5.00. Tel: Worcester (0905) 23221. Celebration of Worcester's famous pottery, factory tours available, shop and restaurant.
TOURIST INFORMATION CENTRE – High Street. Tel: Worcester (0905) 723471. Visit here for full details on other attractions.

### Public Transport

BUSES – Midland Red West services throughout the area and local Citibus services. Tel: Worcester (0905) 23296 & 24898.
TRAINS – stations at Foregate Street and Shrub Hill. Services to/from The Malverns, Birmingham, Kidderminster, and London. Tel: Worcester (0905) 27211.

### Boating Facilities

VIKING AFLOAT – Lowesmoor Wharf, Worcester WR1 2RX. Tel: Worcester (0905) 28667. 2 to 10 berth hire craft. Pumpout, rubbish & Elsan disposal, water, diesel, gas, payphone and souvenir shop. Secure casual moorings.

IF THE SEVERN was a continental river, it would probably be bustling with barges, carrying bulk freight between the ports of the Bristol Channel and the industrial heartlands of Middle England. Once upon a time it fulfilled such a role. Nowadays its the preserve of cabin cruisers, fishing matches and caravan sites. Which is not to say that it is an ugly river – for there are moments when it is profoundly beautiful – but a journey along the forty miles of navigation between Stourport and Gloucester leaves you wishing that the Severn would once again work for its living.

Over two hundred miles long, the Severn is Britain's longest river, and was once considered navigable as far upstream as Welshpool; though such voyages could only be undertaken in favourable conditions, and delays lasting weeks were not unusual if there was not sufficient depth of water in the river. Nevertheless craft traded regularly to Shrewsbury and beyond; partially sailed, and partially hauled by gangs of men. The advent of the Canal Age brought demands for improvements which were characteristically slow to accrue: the hauling men failed to see the humane need for them to be replaced by horses; and Parliamentary bills promoting improvements matched only the barges in their sluggish rate of progress. Not until the coming of the railways did the river interests get their act together. The Severn Horse Towing Path was opened between Bewdley and Worcester in 1804 and a series of locks was built during the middle of that century. but it was all too little, much too late; and river trade went into a spiral of decline as the emergent railways enmeshed the Severn Valley. An Indian Summer of trade followed the opening of oil and petrol depots at Worcester and Stourport which were serviced by tanker barges. But construction of pipelines led to the demise of this trade in the 1960s; just, in final irony, as the locks between Gloucester and Stourport were being mechanised.

**Navigation Authority**
British Waterways
Llanthony Warehouse
Gloucester Docks
Gloucester GL1 2EH
Tel: Gloucester (0452) 25524

**Maximum Dimensions**
Gloucester – Worcester
Length 135ft, beam 22ft, height 24½ft, draught 7½ft.

Worcester – Stourport
Length 89ft, beam 18ft, height 19ft, draught 6ft.

**Lock-keepers Telephone Numbers**
Lincombe Lock – Stourport (02993) 2887
Holt Lock – Worcester (0905) 620218
Bevere Lock – Worcester (0905) 640275
Diglis Lock – Worcester (0905) 354280
Upper Lode Lock – Tewkesbury (0684) 293138

RIVER SEVERN

Upton·upon·Severn

**T**HE SEVERN'S PRESENT head of navigation lies just upstream of Stourport Bridge where the little Gladder Brook enters the river on the west bank. In recent years there have been proposals to restore navigation to the 'Upper Severn', possibly as far as Shrewsbury. David Hutchings, mainspring behind the Upper Avon and Southern Stratford projects, has been linked with these rumours, but nothing concrete has emerged. And indeed, the formal announcement of such a project would be likely to bring in its wake an outburst of protest from conservationists and landowners. In the meantime, if you have a burning desire to explore the river upstream of Stourport you can always proceed on foot, as far perhaps as Bewdley, then on by steam train along the Severn Valley line to Bridgnorth. Alternatively, canoes can be hired from Bridgnorth, paddled down to Bewdley, then taken back on the railway.

Stourport Bridge dates from 1870 and is the third structure to span the river here. The first, designed by James Brindley, was swept contemptuously away by floods in 1794. Stourport might well have become an inland waterway 'crossroads' had the Leominster Canal project fared better than it did. The Act for this 46 mile canal was passed in 1791. Its optimistic promoters envisaged getting rich quick on agricultural exports from the Herefordshire farmlands and industrial imports from the Black Country. A token sod was dug opposite the basins at Stourport in 1797, but the ludicrously ambitious through route was just another still-born enterprise of the Canal Mania, and subsequently, that part of the canal which had been dug, in the vicinity of Tenbury, was converted into a railway. But gosh, wouldn't it have been good to cross the Severn here and voyage off into the wilds of the Abberley Hills and the Teme Valley; another mouth-watering 'might-have-been' in the annals of Britain's canal system.

Like its counterpart Shardlow, built by Brindley where the Trent & Mersey Canal meets the River Trent near Derby, STOURPORT is a canal town par excellence. In 1767, before Brindley began his Staffordshire & Worcestershire Canal, there was nothing here but the small hamlet of Lower Mitton. In the short space of five years a thriving inland port was built. A series of basins, connected to the river by locks, was dug to facilitate transhipment between river vessels and canal boats, and warehouses were built to store goods. Contemporary prints depict a scene of some elegance, dominated by the splendid "Tontine Hotel" (which could once accommodate a hundred guests) and sprinkled

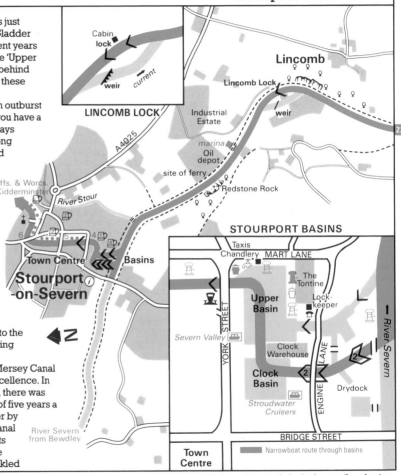

*Estimated time includes lockage to/from basins

with tall-masted trows. Two hundred years later, the inexorable march of time is measured by the sonorous chimes of the clock tower which caps one of the main warehouses. There are still tall masts, whose halyards rattle in the wind, but now they belong to the seagoing yachts which migrate upriver to winter in the security of the basins.

The largest, 'Upper' basin was opened in 1771, and was linked to the Severn through two wide-beam locks, built sturdily enough to withstand the river's propensity for flooding, and capacious enough to take the indigenous Severn trows. A second link with the river, consisting of four narrow-beam locks in staircase pairs, was opened a decade later. These lead up to the 'Clock' basin, overlooked by that handsome warehouse and clock tower which is now used by the local yacht club. There used to be two more basins, east of Mart Lane. They were built early in the 19th century. One was closed in 1866 and a gas works was built on the site. The other flourished in a late period of commercial activity between 1926 and 1949, when narrowboats discharged Cannock and Baggeridge coal here for the power station. The coal was lifted from the boats by electric grab and carried along an aerial ropeway to the power station furnaces. A timber yard covers this basin now, and only a tell-tale 'hump', in an elusive alley leading from Mart Lane to the vinegar brewery, hints at these forgotten docks.

Barely a mile downstream from Stourport lies LINCOMB LOCK, the highest on the river. Boater's acclimatising themselves to the demands of river cruising, may have little time for taking in the scenery, but already the Severn begins to weave its spell on you. One of the high sandstone rockfaces, which periodically rise sheer from the water's edge at various points along the Severn, is encountered almost immediately. Before Stourport Bridge was built there was a ferry here, records of which date back to the 13th century. A hermit is said to have lived in a cave half-way up the rock. Opposite, a well-piled wharf marks the destination of the Severn's last commercial traffics above Worcester. Lincomb Lock lies in a peaceful setting in the early morning shadow of another sandstone outcrop.

## Navigational Advice
Be aware of the possibility of flooding on the Severn – see Information.

When moving between the river and the basins at Stourport take good care in getting on or off the boat to work the locks. The best place to accomplish this is in the entrance to the lowest lock chamber.

## Stourport-on-Severn

Stourport is under the illusion that it is a seaside resort. All the trappings are there – fish & chips, funfairs, amusement arcades, steamer trips and paddling pools – and in the summer trippers pour in from the West Midlands in an attempt to let their hair down and make believe that this is really Rhyl or Weston-super-Mare.

### Eating & Drinking

THE TONTINE (1), built by the canal company as a hotel for merchants and river travellers, is a vast building of immense grace, but would seem unlikely to ever recapture the atmosphere of its heyday. Nevertheless it's the sort of place you'll want to try just to satisfy your curiosity. The beer is Banks's, bar lunches are available on weekdays, and there's an excellent family room. If you like your ale real and rare then try THE HOLLYBUSH (2) which does home-cooking and offers an excellent cycle of guest beers. Other pubs worth considering are THE BLACK STAR (3), Marstons, meals, families catered for, and THE ANGEL (4) Banks's, bar food, riverside. Lots of Indian restaurants too.

### Shopping

A modest selection of shops, plus branches of all the main banks, can be found in the town centre. We found at least one good delicatessen and noticed several decent butchers. The 'Lock Shop' – an old toll house overlooking York Street Lock – is open late, daily and is used to catering for the whimsical needs of dishevelled boaters.

### Things to Do

TOURIST INFORMATION CENTRE – The Library, Worcester Street. Tel: Stourport (02993) 2866.
SEVERN STEAMBOAT CO – Tel: Stourport (02993) 71177. Public trips to Worcester & back, Weds in Jul & Aug. Dep 11am, arr 1.30; leave 4, arr back 6.30pm.
SEVERN VALLEY RAILWAY – Tel: Bewdley (0299) 403816. Steam trains which run, for much of the way, beside the river between Bewdley and Bridgnorth; also a station at Kidderminster.

### Public Transport

BUSES – frequent "Wyre Shuttle" services to/from Kidderminster, plus Midland Red West limited stop services to/from Birmingham & Worcester. Tel: Kidderminster (0562) 823631.

### Boating Facilities

SEVERN VALLEY CRUISERS – York Street, Stourport-on-Severn DY13 9EL. Tel: Stourport (02993) 71165. 2 to 8 berth hire craft (Hoseasons). Pumpout, diesel, gas, servicing & repairs, slipway, boatbuilding, sales & brokerage, crane, moorings. Chandlers shop on Mart Lane.
STROUDWATER CRUISERS – Engine Lane, Stourport-on-Severn DY13 9EP. Tel: Stourport 77222. 2 to 12 berth hire craft (Hoseasons). Pumpout, diesel, gas, moorings, servicing & repairs, crane (up to 7 tons) boatbuilding, sales & brokerage.
STOURPORT MARINA – Tel: Stourport 78012. Large establishment on river primarily concerned with wide beam craft.

"**A**NYONE SO DISPOSED could forget the present in Shrawley Woods" wrote L.T.C. Rolt "(Worcestershire", Robert Hale, 1949), going on to evoke two halcyon summer days moored with *Cressy* along this most beautiful of upper navigable Severn reaches between Lincomb and Holt locks. Disregard for the present presupposes a nostalgia for the past, and it is intriguing to discover that Dick Brook – emerging almost imperceptibly out of the shadowy trees on the western bank – was made navigable in the 17th century to serve a forge located deep in the woods. Two or three lock chambers were cut out of the sandstone, and barges trading up from the Forest of Dean, conveyed cargoes of pig iron along the narrow stream to the doors of the forge.

The Severn acts like a magnet to West Midlanders seeking solace from their urban environment. A rash of caravan parks, and shanty-like chalets mar otherwise unspoilt riverside meadows, for everyone but their proud owners. Luckily, this manifestation of mankind's capacity for destroying the very tranquility he desires, is confined to those parts of the river near main roads. Holt Fleet is such a spot, apt to bristle with 'Brummies' on sunny weekends, and yet Telford's dignified bridge of 1827, the replendent lock, and the tumbling woods on the southern bank, do much to dissipate the crowds. At least the boater can escape up or down stream to more secluded reaches; they, poor sods, have to fight their way through the traffic all the way home.

Before Telford's bridge was built, travellers crossed the river at Holt by ferry. Trace your finger down an old map of the Severn and you'll discover a sad litany of forgotten water crossings between Stourport and Worcester: Redstone, Cloth House, Hampstall, Lenchford, Hawford, Camp, Kepax and Pitchcroft. Alas the idyllic and (to anyone ever charmed by H.G. Wells' account of 'Mr Polly's' sojourn at the "Potwell Inn") enviable lifestyle of the ferrymen came to an end once people replaced Sunday afternoon rambles along the riverbank with an outing by car. Not that there wasn't a darker side to ferrying. In 1919 the Hampstall ferry at The Burf was swamped by the waves of a passing steamer and sank, drowning nine people.

**Eating & Drinking**

THE HAMPSTALL INN – riverside at The Burf. Customer moorings. Bar meals, children catered for, garden.
THE LENCHFORD – riverside 1ml upstream of Holt.
THE HOLT FLEET – south bank by Holt Bridge. Bar meals, limited customer moorings.
THE WHARF – north bank by Holt Bridge. Whitbread/Flowers ales, bar meals, games room, families catered for, payphone.
*There is also a cafe handy by the public moorings at Holt.*

**Shopping**

General stores which sells Calor gas, open daily at Holt Fleet.

**Public Transport**

BUSES – Midland Red West services Mon-Sat to/from Kidderminster and Worcester. Tel: Kidderminster (0562) 823631.

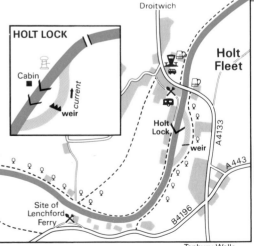

**B**EVERE LOCK is a regular winner in British Waterways' annual 'Best Kept Lock' competition. A high, thick conifer hedge frames the chamber opposite the lock-keeper's cabin and there are flower beds everywhere. All Severn locks seem well cared for, but this one is obviously a labour of love.

Scenically this section of the Severn can best be summed up as 'pleasantly uneventful'. Above Bevere it disappears into the woods for a time; below, it begins to encounter suburban Worcester. Almost opposite the isolated village of Grimley – where Napoleon's brother, Lucien Bonaparte lived for a while in exile – the little River Salwarpe enters the Severn, and is navigable for a short distance by cabin cruisers and the like, up as far as Judge's boatyard. Adjacent, though not so easily discerned, lies the bottom lock of the Droitwich 'Barge' Canal opened in 1771. Surveyed by James Brindley, but actually engineered by John Priddey, the canal flourished during the 19th century as an export route for Droitwich salt. With the decline of this industry, the canal's *raison d'etre* vanished, and it was out of use long before being officially abandoned in 1939. In 1973 a Trust was formed to rescue the canal and a good deal of progress has been made further up the valley, with a trip-boat operating on the summit section. The main hurdle remaining before a connection with the Severn can be achieved, is to somehow get round the embankment laid over the canal bed when the A449 was rebuilt as a dual carriageway.

"Camp House Inn" is an old rivermen's ale house. The bow-haulers would rest here for the night. Sometimes, if the river was too low for them to proceed, they might be stranded here for days; and by all accounts it wasn't long before not only the river was 'dry'. The hauling gangs worked in teams of up to twenty men, each with a chest harness. Contemplated from the viewpoint of our welfare society, it seems incomprehensible that the hauling men opposed 'modernisation' of the Severn, the development of a proper towing path and their replacement by horse power. But they had a living to make, and even if a good proportion of them died early through heart failure, the arduous nature of their work must have seemed less of a threat to them than the loss of their jobs. There is an island in the river at Bevere which is said to have been a refuge place for the Saxon citizens of Worcester when their home town was invaded by the Danes in the 11th century. Later they came here to escape the Bubonic plague.

### Eating & Drinking
CAMP HOUSE INN – riverside below Bevere Lock, moorings for patrons. Pleasant, isolated Whitbread pub where food is usually available except on Sundays. Families catered for. Nice garden.

### Boating Facilities
GEORGE JUDGE – Mill House, Hawford, Worcester. Tel: Worcester (0905) 51283. Pumpout, diesel, water, Elsan & rubbish disposal, Calor gas, repairs & servicing, chandlery, food and cafe during season. Access limited to craft of maximum length 45ft and 3ft draught.

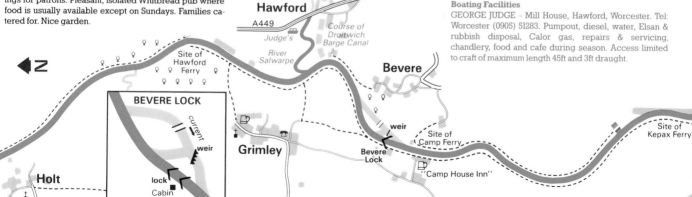

**W**ORCESTER'S RIVERFRONT is dominated by the CATHEDRAL. This image of the great west window, the bulwark of the nave and the high pinnacled tower overlooking a bend in the Severn, forms one of the most wonderful and unmistakeable provincial views of England. On no other navigation do you rub shoulders quite so intimately with an ecclesiastical masterpiece.

A FERRY operates across the river in the vicinity of the cathedral on summer weekends, carrying King's schoolboys across to their playing fields, spectators to the gorgeous New Road cricket ground, and people who just enjoy the sensation of crossing the river by such romantic means. The 'Cathedral Ferry' has its roots in the 13th century but the present operation dates from as recently as 1981. Use of the ferry had lapsed in the Sixties, so a group got together to breath new life into the old tradition. They found a suitable clinker-built rowing boat languishing in the South Coast town of Bridport, had it brought up to Worcester, and named it *Doris* after a local benefactress; traditionally the ferry boat had been called *Betty* in memory of an 18th century ferry lady.

Two bridges span the Severn at Worcester. The busy, and not unattractive, road bridge has five stone arches. This particular structure dates from 1781; though it was widened in the Thirties. The more ornate and loftier railway bridge carries the beautiful line to Hereford out of Foregate Street station on its way to the Malverns. North of the railway crossing, along the east bank, extends the PITCHCROFT, a public amenity of long standing which incorporates Worcester's race course. At the north end of this is Pitchcroft Boating Station, from which rowing and motor boats can be hired.

Converted warehouses line the east bank south of WORCESTER BRIDGE. They recall a time when the waterfront was busy with river traffic. A regular trader to Worcester was the steam coaster *Atlanta*, built at Bristol in 1884 and purchased by the Severn & Canal Carrying Company a decade later. She would bring cargoes up from the Bristol Channel ports and tranship them into narrowboats below the bridge; for, with a beam of 19½ft, she was too wide to gain access to Diglis Basin.

Less than half a mile downstream from the Cathedral stands the entrance lock to DIGLIS BASIN and the Worcester & Birmingham Canal. Nearby is DIGLIS RIVER LOCK which has paired chambers; that on the east bank being the smaller of the two.

### Navigational Advice
As at Stourport, taking crew on board or letting them off to work the canal locks is not always easy at Diglis. One of the easiest access points is the sanitary station pontoon moored just downstream of the canal entrance. A ladder leads from this to *terra firma*.

### Moorings
Formal moorings on the river are limited to the steamer quay on the east bank between the rail and road bridges, and the old oil dock above the river lock. For maximum security, and freedom from worries over any fluctuation in river levels, lock up into Diglis Basins.

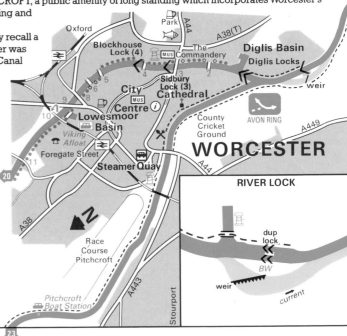

A MODERN, and inevitably concrete, road bridge takes Worcester's southern by-pass over the river half a mile south of its confluence with the Teme. Like a deferential waitress, coming in to clear the dishes, the Teme makes little impact on the haughty Severn. But on its way down from the Welsh Marches, past Ludlow and through the hopyards of Herefordshire, this lovely river hits heights of beauty that the Severn arguably never attains.

Our old chum William Sandys (see River Avon) acquired the rights to make the Teme navigable up to Ludlow in the 17th century, but he never got around to actually doing anything about it. Perhaps the Civil War got in his way. Just a stone's throw from here the first skirmish of that conflict took place at Powick Bridge on the 23rd of September 1642. The Parliamentarians lost that battle, but ironically enough, won the war by defeating the Royalist forces on virtually the same battlefield nine years later.

South of Worcester the Severn pursues an undemonstrative course. Below Kempsey travellers heading downstream begin to get glimpses of the Malvern Hills beyond the Severn's high, and it has to be said, somewhat dull banks. But if the scenery momentarily falters, the novelty of deep and wide water has yet to wear off. Coming out of the confines of the canal at Worcester is like leaving school and all its petty impositions behind for the summer holidays. And unless you are braving the Severn out of season, as likely as not there'll be a fair amount of boat traffic about. Narrow boats begin to look a bit out of place amongst all these floating gin palaces. But everyone, it seems, is in a mood of bonhomie, and it's the done thing to acknowledge each passing vessel with a cheerful wave.

KEMPSEY comes bravely down to the riverbank, but the passing boater sees little more than a long line of pontoon moorings belonging to the local boatyard. The A38 trunk road bisects the village and a good deal of modern housing has expanded around the core of the original settlement. Old maps mark the site of a 'Bishop's Palace' and apparently royal visits were two a penny here in the middle ages. Simon de Montfort stopped off with his prisoner, Henry III, before the Battle of Evesham in 1265. The Ham was used for military reviews and also confrontations of a more personal nature, the last recorded duel in the county taking place here in 1827.

An old ferry house marks the site of a former river crossing at PIXHAM. In his informative account of fords and ferries on the Severn in Worcestershire (published locally in 1982), H.W. Gwilliam relates that the ferry here was capable of carrying motor vehicles until it ceased operating around the time of the second world war. It seems that there was no formal road approach to the ferry stage on the Kempsey side, so cars had to be driven across the field as best they could. The local hunt used the ferry as well and it must have been some sight to see the hounds packed aboard the vessel for the river crossing.

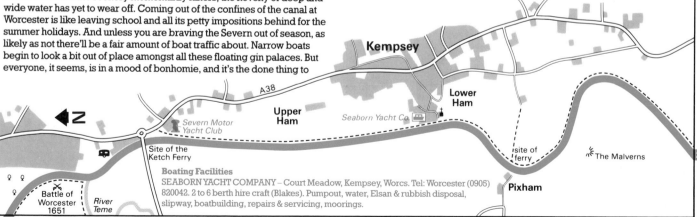

**Boating Facilities**

SEABORN YACHT COMPANY – Court Meadow, Kempsey, Worcs. Tel: Worcester (0905) 820042. 2 to 6 berth hire craft (Blakes). Pumpout, water, Elsan & rubbish disposal, slipway, boatbuilding, repairs & servicing, moorings.

**U**NDER THE WATCHFUL EYE of the Malverns, the River Severn winds past occasional outcrops of sandstone rock; welcome interludes of drama amid the monotony of the willow-lined banks. This is probably the prettiest part of the river between Worcester and Tewkesbury, and though there are few formal moorings, owners of light draughted cabin cruisers seem prepared to tie up to overhanging tree trunks and enjoy a peaceful picnic. CLEVELODE is a pleasant little community of orchards and cottages, but just downstream lies one of those caravan sites which the Severn seems fated to attract. There were ferries both here and at RHYDD. The sandstone outcrop extended across the bed of the river and caused problems with navigation before the locks were built.

If the rocky bluffs have a Rhineish quality about them, then, in the context of the Severn Plain, the Malverns are positively Alpine. They are the highest point along the 52 latitude between the Black Mountains of Wales and the Harz Mountains in Germany. It is impossible not be moved by their brooding presence. They were the inspiration behind much of Sir Edward Elgar's music, though the Severn also played a part in exciting his muse. "I am still at heart the dreamy child who used to be found in the reeds by Severn side with a sheet of paper, trying to fix the sounds and longing for something great." Caught once at rehearsal for a way to convey his intentions, he told the orchestra to "play it like something you hear down by the river."

An ostentatious, castellated mansion towers above the woods at SEVERN BANK and an old boat house stands on the west bank of the river below SEVERN END, but there is barely any trace of the former quay at HANLEY CASTLE. Before the roads were metalled and motor lorries appeared on the scene, isolated villages like these would have relied on the river for transport. Coal was brought in by barge and local agricultural produce taken away.

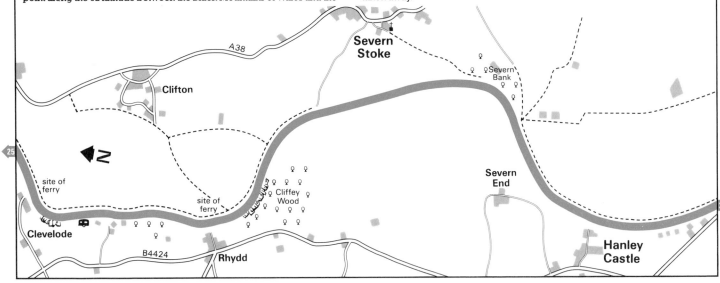

**T**WO ROAD BRIDGES span this section of the Severn. The present bridge at UPTON dates from the second world war. It replaced a swing bridge, the abutments of which can still be seen. Each plod along the road of Progress rids us of something worthwhile. Fords give way to ferries, ferries to swing-bridges, swing-bridges to fixed structures devoid of all character. And now we can travel so quickly that the average journey makes no impression upon us whatsoever. In his book about the county, published in 1949, Tom Rolt described how the old watermen were in the habit of lingering in the cutwater embrassures of the old stone bridge: "smoking, yarning, gazing down at the smoothly flowing water, or watching the activity on the wharves." No-one has the time or inclination to lean over the parapet of the present bridge with its constant stream of traffic. But, for all that, Upton is a delightful town, redolent of those river ghosts of days gone by, and an almost obligatory stop for boaters if, that is, they can find a space to moor.

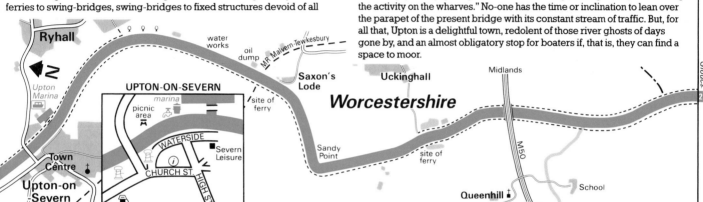

### Upton-on-Severn

The spirit of the Severn pervades this charming little town, giving it the atmosphere of a small coastal port; an illusion enhanced by the semblance of the cupola topped old church tower to a lighthouse.

#### Eating & Drinking

CROMWELLS – Church Street. Bistro and coffee shop.
THE SWAN – Waterside. Well appointed riverside inn. Excellent bar and restaurant food.
UPTON MUGGERY – Old Street. Typically eccentric 'Little Pub Co' establishment. Free mug if you order a Cow Pie.

#### Shopping

All the usual facilities; early closing on Thursdays. Lloyds and Midland banks. Fascinating specialist map shop in the High Street.

#### Things to Do

HERITAGE CENTRE – Old Church Tower. Splendid small museum devoted to Upton's crowded history. Also acts as Tourist Information Centre. Tel: Upton (06846) 4200.
MIDSUMMER WEAVERS – London Lane. Open Tue-Sat. Featuring 'Bertha' and 'George', two quinquagenarian looms which visitors can see in operation. Natural fibre fabrics on sale and a made to measure service. Tel: Upton (06846) 3503.
SEVERN LEISURE CRUISES – Waterside. Tel: Upton (06846) 3112. Public and charter river trips aboard the MV *Conway Castle*. Public trips between Upton and Tewkesbury on Wednesdays Jun-Sep.

#### Public Transport

BUSES – Midland Red West Mon-Sat service to/from Worcester & Gloucester via Tewkesbury. Tel: (0345) 212 555. Also some local buses to/from Malvern, a worthwhile excursion, ask at the TIC for up to date details.

#### Boating Facilities

UPTON MARINA – Upton-on-Severn, Worcs WR8 0PB. Tel: Upton (06846) 3111. Water, diesel, Elsan & rubbish disposal, slipway, Calor gas, drydock, repairs & servicing, moorings & chandlery.
CORSAIR CRUISERS – address as above. Tel: Upton (06846) 3400. 2 to 8 berth wide-beam cruisers for hire.
STARLINE NARROWBOATS – base address as above. Tel: Upton (06846) 3443. Office on Malvern (0684) 574774. 4 to 8 berth hire craft. Pumpout and Calor gas.

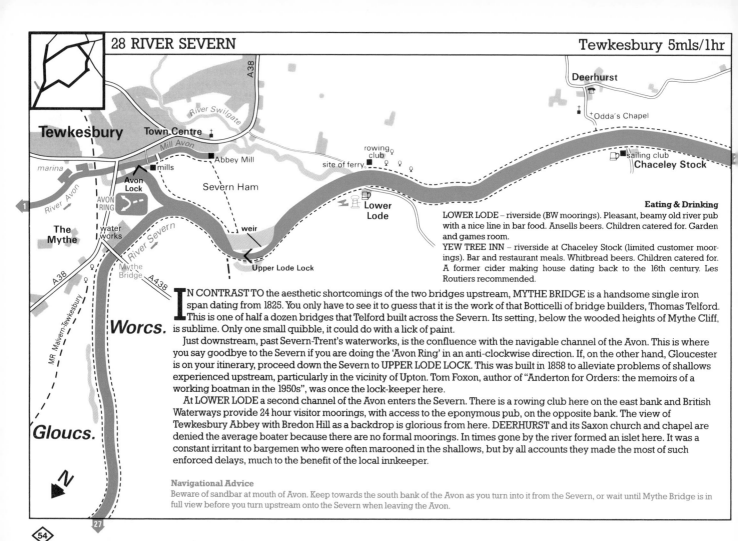

**Eating & Drinking**

LOWER LODE – riverside (BW moorings). Pleasant, beamy old river pub with a nice line in bar food. Ansells beers. Children catered for. Garden and games room.

YEW TREE INN – riverside at Chaceley Stock (limited customer moorings). Bar and restaurant meals. Whitbread beers. Children catered for. A former cider making house dating back to the 16th century. Les Routiers recommended.

IN CONTRAST TO the aesthetic shortcomings of the two bridges upstream, MYTHE BRIDGE is a handsome single iron span dating from 1825. You only have to see it to guess that it is the work of that Botticelli of bridge builders, Thomas Telford. This is one of half a dozen bridges that Telford built across the Severn. Its setting, below the wooded heights of Mythe Cliff, is sublime. Only one small quibble, it could do with a lick of paint.

Just downstream, past Severn-Trent's waterworks, is the confluence with the navigable channel of the Avon. This is where you say goodbye to the Severn if you are doing the 'Avon Ring' in an anti-clockwise direction. If, on the other hand, Gloucester is on your itinerary, proceed down the Severn to UPPER LODE LOCK. This was built in 1858 to alleviate problems of shallows experienced upstream, particularly in the vicinity of Upton. Tom Foxon, author of "Anderton for Orders: the memoirs of a working boatman in the 1950s", was once the lock-keeper here.

At LOWER LODE a second channel of the Avon enters the Severn. There is a rowing club here on the east bank and British Waterways provide 24 hour visitor moorings, with access to the eponymous pub, on the opposite bank. The view of Tewkesbury Abbey with Bredon Hill as a backdrop is glorious from here. DEERHURST and its Saxon church and chapel are denied the average boater because there are no formal moorings. In times gone by the river formed an islet here. It was a constant irritant to bargemen who were often marooned in the shallows, but by all accounts they made the most of such enforced delays, much to the benefit of the local innkeeper.

**Navigational Advice**

Beware of sandbar at mouth of Avon. Keep towards the south bank of the Avon as you turn into it from the Severn, or wait until Mythe Bridge is in full view before you turn upstream onto the Severn when leaving the Avon.

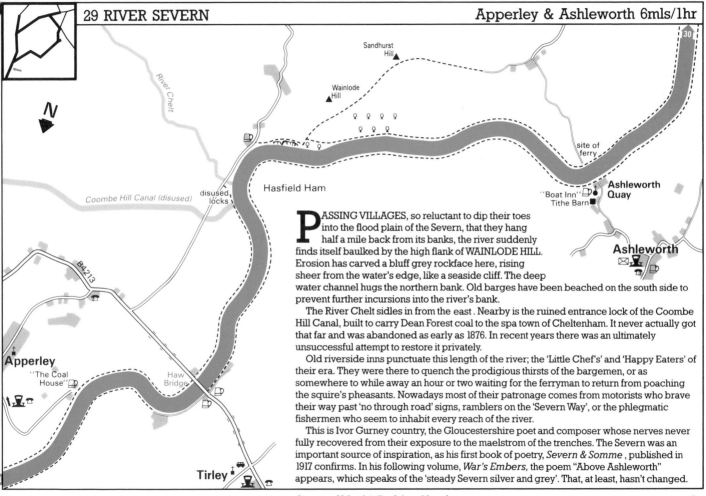

**P**ASSING VILLAGES, so reluctant to dip their toes into the flood plain of the Severn, that they hang half a mile back from its banks, the river suddenly finds itself baulked by the high flank of WAINLODE HILL. Erosion has carved a bluff grey rockface here, rising sheer from the water's edge, like a seaside cliff. The deep water channel hugs the northern bank. Old barges have been beached on the south side to prevent further incursions into the river's bank.

The River Chelt sidles in from the east . Nearby is the ruined entrance lock of the Coombe Hill Canal, built to carry Dean Forest coal to the spa town of Cheltenham. It never actually got that far and was abandoned as early as 1876. In recent years there was an ultimately unsuccessful attempt to restore it privately.

Old riverside inns punctuate this length of the river; the 'Little Chef's' and 'Happy Eaters' of their era. They were there to quench the prodigious thirsts of the bargemen, or as somewhere to while away an hour or two waiting for the ferryman to return from poaching the squire's pheasants. Nowadays most of their patronage comes from motorists who brave their way past 'no through road' signs, ramblers on the 'Severn Way', or the phlegmatic fishermen who seem to inhabit every reach of the river.

This is Ivor Gurney country, the Gloucestershire poet and composer whose nerves never fully recovered from their exposure to the maelstrom of the trenches. The Severn was an important source of inspiration, as his first book of poetry, *Severn & Somme* , published in 1917 confirms. In his following volume, *War's Embers,* the poem "Above Ashleworth" appears, which speaks of the 'steady Severn silver and grey'. That, at least, hasn't changed.

*See page 60 for details of riverside pubs.*

LONG REACH leads to Upper Parting. These old river names have a evocative resonance. And there were deeper subtleties: the navigable channel downstream of the parting was known to working boatmen as 'Skipper's Length', whilst that above was known as 'Mates'. The tradition being that barge skippers would be at the wheel for the tortuous, narrow exit channel from Gloucester, being relieved, once Upper Parting had been reached, by the mate. Statistically, it comes as some surprise to learn that trade on the Severn was at its peak just after the second world war. The carriage of petroleum accounted for the bulk of this. Shell and BP products were carried aboard Harkers tanker barges from Swansea to Worcester; Regent had their own fleet which traded between Avonmouth and Stourport.

The now unnavigable western channel of the Severn, which loops past the village of Maisemore was used to gain access to the Herefordshire & Gloucestershire Canal, a 34 mile rural waterway which took fifty years to build, and which within forty years of its completion in 1845 had largely been converted into a railway.

The navigable, eastern channel of the Severn must have demanded all the barge skipper's fund of experience. If you have been used to the motorway breadth of the river down from Tewkesbury, this B road backwater comes as something of a shock. It forms a surreptitious approach to the city, for the overhanging willows hide any view which might otherwise be had of the cathedral. Presently a series of bridges span the river as roads and railways converge on the city centre. A final zig and a final zag reveals the long high wall of the old River Quay where, before development of the docks and the ship canal from Sharpness, vessels which had navigated up the tidal Severn would berth.

Downstream of the Quay the river branches again, the right hand channel leads round to Lower Parting and is no longer navigable. Once, back in the mists of time, coal boats from the Forest of Dean used this route. During the last war a coaster brought coal from Barry in South Wales to the power station jetty opposite here. There was insufficient room to turn the vessel after it had discharged its cargo, and so it had to be manoeuvered backwards into the lock and turned in the Main Basin.

GLOUCESTER LOCK dates from 1812 and was originally in the form of a staircase pair. Now it is one, fairly deep chamber, mechanised and spanned by a swingbridge carrying a road busy with heavy lorries in an arc around the western perimeter of the docks. Only the most narrow-minded canal enthusiast could fail to experience a surge of excitement as the lock fills and GLOUCESTER DOCKS are gradually revealed in all their grandeur. The sight of the wide expanse of the Main Basin, set like a stage against the theatrical backdrop of the huge, brick warehouses, generates the sort of buzz of anticipation you feel before the curtain rises on some glittering production you'd promised to treat yourself to for a long time. So it is with a sense of exhilaration that you proceed out of the lock to secure a berth amidst such splendid surroundings.

Since the demise of the last commercial traffics in the early 1980s, the basins have become a centre of pleasure boating, whilst the warehouses have been refurbished as offices, flats, restaurants and museums. Such regeneration is not unique. London, Liverpool, Bristol and Hull have all waved a magic wand over similarly decaying dockscapes, but this is the only dockland redevelopment linked directly to the inland waterways system, and it is doubly appropriate that it has become the site of the National Waterways Museum. And what better, more fitting, way to visit this than having navigated down the Severn?

Gloucester was given the formal status of a port way back in Elizabeth I's time. But the Severn was always a difficult river to navigate and trade didn't blossom to extent it might have done had access been easier. To overcome these problems a ship canal was promoted at the end of the 18th century to by-pass the worst sections of the Severn; and though delayed by the Napoleonic Wars, the Gloucester & Berkeley (later Sharpness) Canal was finally opened in 1827. The timing couldn't have been bettered. Britain was in the grip of the Industrial Revolution and soon those investors who had persevered with the long, drawn out construction of the canal were laughing all the way to the bank. Tall-masted brigs, schooners and barques laden with timber from Russia and North America, wine from France and Portugal and corn from Ireland began to fill the basin. A major export trade developed with Droitwich salt, brought down the Severn in trows and transhipped into larger vessels in the basin here. In his marvellously detailed illustrated history ("Gloucester Docks", Alan Sutton 1988), Hugh Conway-Jones describes the development of the docks in illuminating detail. The earliest archive photographs of them date from the late 1860s and have a Long John Silverish quality which makes you eager for a time machine. No wonder the makers of the "Onedin Line" television series did so much work on location here back in the 1970s.

Gloucester Docks were at their zenith in the age of sail, remained busy through the steam era, but declined when different trading patterns emerged as vessels began to grow too large to use the ship canal. Around 1982, Healings ceased the regular carriage of grain from Avonmouth and Sharpness up to their flour mill at Tewkesbury, though their fleet of barges remain in good repair, berthed on the Avon beside the mills, so that they could be used again if ever required. The mid Eighties also saw the end of

→

## Navigational Advice

The approach off the Severn and into Gloucester Lock needs considerable care and attention. The current draws craft towards the unnavigable channel to Lower Parting which has a WEIR a quarter of a mile downstream from here. There are chains and ladders recessed on the Quay wall to your left. Loop a line through one of these until the green light signals that you can enter the lock. On entering the lock the keeper will probably lower a hook down to you to loop your line through. He will loop this over the nearest bollard and then return the other end to you, so that the boat can be steadied against any turbulence as the lock fills.

## Moorings

Refer to enlargement for location of casual moorings within the docks. Ask the lock-keeper for further details.

### KEY

1. Custom House
2. Priday & Metford flour mill
3. North Warehouse
4. Lock Warehouse (antiques)
5. Victoria Warehouse
6. Herbert Warehouse
7. Kimberley Warehouse
8. Phillpotts Warehouse
9. Brittania Warehouse
10. Albert Warehouse (Opie Mus)
11. Vinings Warehouse
12. Reynolds Warehouse
13. Shipton & Biddle Warehouses
14. Llanthony Warehouse (Mus)
15. Alexandra Warehouse (BW)

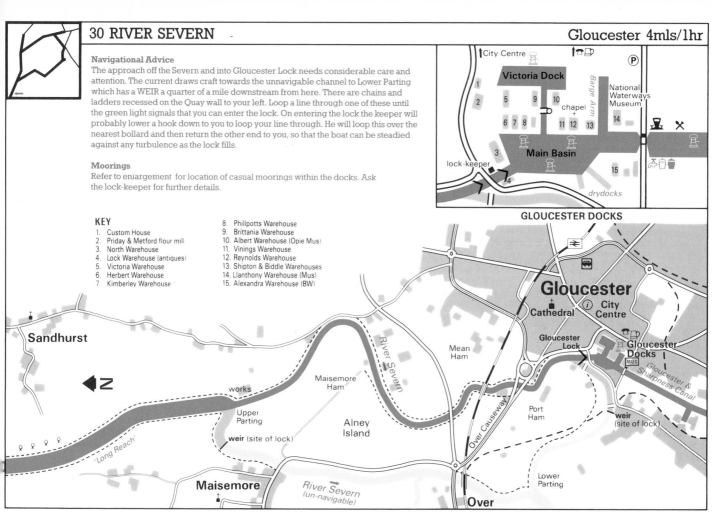

GLOUCESTER DOCKS

oil traffic on the Gloucester & Sharpness Canal and nowadays visits of coasters to the quays south of Llanthony lift bridge are rare events. To all intents and purposes, Gloucester Docks, like the Severn itself, have no commercial significance; though they continue to be categorised as commercial waterways by British Waterways.

So there you have it. We have journeyed down all the forty odd miles of the navigable Severn. It has been a voyage through time as well as space.

Dusk is gathering over the haunted waters of the Main Basin. The cathedral tower looms above the rooftop of the dock office, the last lorry has left the flour mill for the night, and the sun has set over the Forest of Dean. Voices echo across the twinkling expanse of water, floodlights splash warm arcs of brightness on the brickwork of the shadowy warehouses. The setting is superb, rivalling Gas Street Basin and Wigan Pier in being amongst the best urban canal moorings in the country. Goodnight.

## Gloucester

Charles Dickens was amazed to find merchant seamen wandering conspicuously along the streets of what he had imagined would be a quiet cathedral city. He followed one and discovered "endless intricacies of dock...and huge three-masted ships". Of course there are no sailors to be followed nowadays and, in any case, one has one's reputation to consider. Also, most users of this guidebook will be wondering what Gloucester *itself* is like, having already become acquainted with the docks. In fact, it's a bit of a curate's egg, a bit of a Mahler symphony; being made up of serene passages and alleyways skirting the cathedral close, interspersed with strident streets and concrete shopping precincts. Here and there is evidence of the Roman 'Glevum', stressing Gloucester's longevity. But, as an entity, the city suffers from a lack of homogeneity; each age having despoilt just enough of its heritage to render the whole thing too piecemeal for its own good. Gloucester has, however, in its cathedral, a masterpiece of medieval architecture, an act of faith which spans milleniums and transcends the shortcomings of the modern day city. Here is the largest stained glass window in England, the tomb of King Edward II and, in one shadowy corner, a memorial to a battalion of the Gloucestershire Regiment who made an heroic stand against all odds during an incident in the Korean War.

### Eating & Drinking

Two pubs by the dock gate on Southgate Street are: the down-to-earth WATERSMITH'S ARMS (Flowers, Arkells, snacks, basket meals) and the more upmarket TALL SHIP (Wadworth, bar and restaurant meals). Dockside, downstream of Llanthony lift bridge is SWEENEY TODD'S cafe restaurant housed in a converted warehouse; you can moor outside the door. Two restaurants worth considering in the city centre are: THE ENGLISH HOUSE RE-

STAURANT on Worcester Street which specialises in traditional English food (Tel: Gloucester 300772) and THE NEW INN, a 15th century Berni Inn (!) with a remarkable courtyard.

### Shopping

All the household names can be found in the Eastgate Shopping Centre. The excellent market is open daily except, of course, for Sundays. There are some useful 'corner-shops' in the vicinity of the docks on Southgate Street and Llanthony Road. GLOUCESTER ANTIQUE CENTRE is apparently second only to the cathedral as a tourist attraction. It is housed in the former Lock Warehouse. The ground floor is devoted to large items of furniture, whilst the upper floors consist of a series of 'Dickensian' arcades.

### Things to Do

TOURIST INFORMATION CENTRE – The Cross. Tel (0452) 421188.

THE NATIONAL WATERWAYS MUSEUM – Llanthony Warehouse, Gloucester Docks, Gloucester GL1 2EH. Tel: Gloucester (0452) 307009. Open daily. Admission charge. British Waterways' showpiece museum housed in one of the handsome dockside warehouses. Excellent indoor displays. Outdoor floating exhibits include a steam dredger, narrowboats and barges.

MUSEUM OF ADVERTISING & PACKAGING – Albert Warehouse, Gloucester Docks, Gloucester GL1 2EH. Tel: Gloucester (0452) 302309. Open daily ex Mons. Admission charge. A perfect compliment to the Waterways Museum, Robert Opie's collection of yesteryear tins, packets, boxes and bottles takes us all back to the pre-supermarket era of "Camp" Coffee, 'Five Boys' chocolate, and Borwick's baking powder.

HOUSE OF THE TAILOR OF GLOUCESTER – 9 College Court, Gloucester GL1 2NJ. Tel: Gloucester (0452) 422856. Open Mon-Sat. Delightful shop and museum devoted to the world of Beatrix Potter, who used this actual house as a model for her famous children's story about the mice who made the mayor's waistcoat.

FOLK MUSEUM – Westgate St, Gloucester GL1 2PG. Tel: Gloucester (0452) 26467. Open Mon-Sat. Marvellous collection of Gloucestershire bygones housed in handsome half-timbered premises.

CITY MUSEUM & ART GALLERY – Brunswick Road, Gloucester GL1 1HP. Tel: (0452) 24131. Open Mon-Sat. Antiques, art and Roman remains.

### Public Transport

BUSES – services throughout the city and county. Tel Gloucester (0452) 425543.

TRAINS – excellent railhead. Tel: Gloucester (0452) 29501.

continued from Map 4

Birmingham. If you are cruising the Avon Ring you will meet it again in happier circumstances at Alvechurch, on the Worcester & Birmingham Canal.

Glass houses, glinting in the sunlight, emphasise Evesham's reputation as a fruit growing centre, as the river skirts its western suburbs and you pass the flourishing ferry at HAMPTON. This is one of only two public ferries still in existence on the Avon. It provides a popular short cut for the housewives of Hampton to reach Evesham's shops. There is an aesthetic pleasure in its toing and froing which makes you sad that not more of the river's ferries have survived.

A stately bridge, named after one of the town's Victorian mayors, spans the Avon in the centre of Evesham, and recreation grounds, bordered by avenue of limes, create a gracious riverside environment. We spent a couple of hot August days here amongst the shirt-sleeved crowds,and there were images which reminded us of Seurat's famous pointillistic masterpiece of the Ile de la Grande-Jatte. EVESHAM LOCK is the highest upstream on the Lower Avon. It is manned and mechanised. Mr White, the lock-keeper, is a friendly soul who once worked on the Mersey ferries. His wife runs a small shop in one room of their unusual, triangular-shaped house which spans the old chamber of the original lock. Their dog, 'Dino' is being trained as lock assistant. He's pretty good with the ropes, but has yet to master the balance beams. Evesham mill is now used by the local meat factory as a social club.

Between Evesham and OFFENHAM the river is left pretty much to its own devices. The railway and the by-pass cross the Avon but leave little impression upon it. Beyond the water-meadows, and the likelihood of floods, the countryside is thick with regimented fruit trees. Deadman's Ait was the scene of heavy fighting during the Battle of Evesham. Many Welshmen were slaughtered here, and large quantities of human remains were unearthed during the eighteenth century. The peace we associate with the English landscape had to be fought for.

## Cropthorne

A peaceful village situated on a hill overlooking the Avon. No pub within easy walking distance of the river but a useful post office stores easily reached from the private house mooring by Jubilee Bridge.

## Fladbury

Quiet residential village where you get the distinct impression that they like to 'keep themselves to themselves'. Nearest moorings are at the private house by Jubilee Bridge. From there it's about half a mile along the road to the village centre where you'll find a pub, butcher, post office and village stores which does hot snacks and which stocks a reasonable choice of wines.

## Evesham

The name sounds so mellifluous that one expects romantic things of Evesham. A town at the centre of such a fruity, fecund vale should be correspondingly ripe with charm. But even the by-pass hasn't saved Evesham's streets from its surfeit of road traffic, and this problem serves to blight the otherwise handsome thoroughfares of the town. Perhaps if you arrive here by car it doesn't seem so bad, but boaters are not used to such hustle and bustle, and half an hour's exposure to this is apt to send you scurrying back to the river's relative calm. First, though, you must see the best of Evesham. The Bell Tower, for example, which is all that is left of an abbey demolished after the Dissolution (Interesting, isn't it, that Tewkesbury Abbey survived intact, Pershore Abbey lost just its nave, and yet Evesham Abbey was demolished entirely, apart from this tower!). The carillon here is considered (locally at any rate) amongst the best half dozen in the world. Two spires provide counterpoint to the tower's dominating bulk. Nearby is The Almonry, housing the town's small museum, which includes a model showing the extent of the original abbey. One further building of antiquity is the Round House in the Market Place, a sprawling, half timbered structure dating from 1450, which isn't remotely circular. It houses the Nat West bank.

### Eating & Drinking

THE LANTERN EATING HOUSE – Bridge Street (west of Workman Bridge). Old fashioned cafe/restaurant for inexpensive family meals.

THE VAUXHALL – Merstow Green (opposite TIC) 'Beafeater' steak bar.

THE VINE INN – opposite above. Wine bar with good choice of vegetarian dishes on the menu.

THE TRUMPET – Merstow Green. Bass, bar lunches (ex Sun).

RIVERSIDE RESTAURANT – Upriver from town adjacent to by-pass bridge. Tel: Evesham (0386) 446200. Customer moorings.

### Shopping

Full facilities on west bank of river, market on Saturdays. Evesham is reasonably well endowed with familiar chain stores such as W.H. Smith and Woolworths. Handy local shops in the suburb of Bengeworth, east of Workman Bridge.

### Things to Do

THE ALMONRY – 14th century building now used as TOURIST INFORMATION CENTRE and local history museum. Tel: Evesham (0386) 6944.

### Public Transport

BUSES – Midland Red West throughout the Vale of Evesham. Tel: (0345) 212555.

TRAINS – Cotswold Line services to/from Worcester, Oxford and Paddington. Tel: Worcester (0905) 27211.

## Offenham

A straggling village surrounded by line upon line of hothouses. The moorings and ferry belong to the BRIDGE INN, a friendly M&B house which usually does food. A couple of miles upstream (Map 5) lies the FISH & ANCHOR (beside George Billington Lock) a rambling fisherman's pub serving M&B beers and bar meals.

Other places to visit include: TEWKESBURY ABBEY; THE LITTLE MUSEUM; OLD BAPTIST CHAPEL and BATTLE OF TEWKESBURY Waymarked Trail. Contact the TIC for full details.

The following companies operate trip boats and/or hire out motor launches: TIME & TIDE, Mill Avon, Tel: Tewkesbury (0684) 298730; TEWKESBURY BOAT CENTRE, Mill Avon, Tel: Tewkesbury (0684) 294023; SEVERN LEISURE CRUISES, King John's Island South, Tel: Upton (06846) 3112 or 2988.

### Public Transport
BUSES – Cheltenham & District to/from Cheltenham. Tel: Cheltenham (0242) 522021. Midland Red West to/from Worcester, Upton and Gloucester. Tel: Worcester (0905) 24898.

### Twyning Green
Charming riverside village with wide green. Two pubs; one – THE FLEET INN – with very limited moorings.

### Bredon
This is John Moore's *Brensham*. The 14th century Tithe Barn is open to the public (Mar-Nov, Wed, Thur, Sat & Sun) under the aegis of the National Trust. Bredon has many delightful buildings, two stores, two pubs and a riverside car park, *but no public moorings!* BREDON DOCK provide private moorings for cabin cruisers, telephone (0684) 72795 for further details.

### Shopping
The town bristles with quality shops engaged in the business of emptying the bank accounts of visitors. But many of these shops have such character that you don't resent being fleeced. Even the chain stores, like Marks & Spencer in Bridge Street, appear to have more flair than branches elsewhere. The best policy, chaps, is to get here after the shops have shut and insist – use what excuse you like – on an early start. PS, Market day is on Fridays.

### Things to Do
There are far too many individual attractions to list here. They range from the obvious to the esoteric; from SHAKESPEARE'S BIRTHPLACE to the TEDDY BEAR MUSEUM. Everything you ever wanted to know but were reluctant to ask can be discovered at the TOURIST INFORMATION CENTRE on the corner of High and Bridge streets. Tel: Stratford (0789) 293127. If you do nothing else try and catch a perfomance at one of the theatres; visit the box office by the Canal Basin or telephone ahead on Stratford (0789) 295623.

### Public Transport
BUSES – Midland Red South services to all parts of the region. Tel: Rugby (0788) 535555.

TRAINS – good connections with Birmingham and Leamington Spa. Tel: 021-643 2711.

### Eating & Drinking
THE COAL HOUSE – riverside, Apperley (BW moorings due to be installed 1990). Likeable one-room pub. Wide choice of beer including their own 'Floodwater' bitter (actually Hall's keg!), Wadworth, Hook Norton and regular guests. Good menu, highlight of which is 'Steak on the Stone'. Children catered for.
HAW BRIDGE INN – riverside, Haw Bridge (BW moorings). Whitbread, food, garden.
THE NEW INN – riverside, Haw Bridge. Youngers, food, garden.
BOAT INN – riverside, Ashleworth Quay (mooring not easy but worth improvising). A wonderful survival, completely timeless and unspoilt, this little pub is run by two sisters. Bread and cheese is occasionally available but there's no attempt at formal catering. Not that you need to eat here, just quaff your beer and immerse yourself in the unostentacious atmosphere and the ladies' lilting Gloucestershire dialect. Nice old sign for Bathhurst's boatyard at Tewkesbury behind the bar. Beer (straight from the barrel) includes Arkells and Flowers. Just up the often flooded lane is a beautiful stone built tithe barn. Open formally to the public during the summer under the auspices of the National Trust, but informally in the winter; if you don't mind sharing it with the sheep.

# Information

## How to Use the Maps

There are thirty numbered maps covering the following waterways:

River Avon 1 – 7
Stratford Canal 8 – 13
Worcester & Birmingham Canal 14 – 20
River Severn 21 – 30

If you are using this Companion to guide you around the AVON RING in an anti-clockwise direction – no matter from where you start – you should read the maps from left to right; travelling clockwise, you read right to left. For example, if you were to travel from Bidford in a clockwise direction, you would turn first to Map 6, then 5 etc to 1; then Map 28, 27 etc to 24; then 20, 19 etc to 13; then 12, 11 etc back to 6. If you intend staying religiously on the 'ring', there is no need to refer to Maps 14, 21-23 and 29 & 30 as these cover connecting routes. In any case, the simplest way of progressing from map to map is to proceed to the next map numbered from the edge of the map you are on. Any questions?

A 'thumbnail' diagram at the top left hand corner of each map indicates your overall position. Figures quoted at the top of each map refer to distance and average cruising time for that particular page. An alternative indication of mileages and times can be found on the Route Planner inside the front cover. Obviously cruising times vary with the nature of your boat and the number of crew at your disposal, so quoted times should only be taken as an estimate and not as a challenge.

## Using the Text

Each map is accompanied by a route commentary describing the landscape and placing the waterway in its historical context. Brief portraits of canal and riverside towns and villages are given together with itemised or summarised information on facilities.

## Eating & Drinking.

Pubs, restaurants, cafes, fish & chip shops and fast-food outlets considered to be of interest to users of this guide are listed. In towns and cities a selection obviously has to be made, so we try and list a cross-section of establishments likely to appeal to different tastes and budgets. We don't set out to make judgements in an 'Egon Ronay' sense, but, generally speaking, the more detail we give, the higher in esteem any particular establishment is likely to be held. by the very nature of their trade, pubs and restaurants have a tendency to change hands, alter their services, or simply close down, and we apologise in advance for any misleading entries in the text. Let us know about them and we'll endeavour to correct them in the next edition.

## Shopping.

Shopping in unfamiliar towns and villages is one of the pleasures of boating. In the case of larger places we try to give an impression of the style and nature of the facilities available, mentioning any particularly interesting or charming shops which caught our eye, whilst with regard to villages we list what's available in basic detail. Locating shops is made easy by reference to the symbols on the maps.

## Things to Do.

Details are given in this category of Tourist Information Centres, museums, stately homes etc likely to be of interest to users of the guide.

## Public Transport.

Information in this category is quoted for the benefit of walkers wishing to walk 'one-way', using the bus or train in the opposite direction. It may also be of use to boaters planning an excursion 'ashore'. We advise you to use the telephone number quoted to check service details.

## Boating Facilities.

Every boatyard and hirebase is marked on the relevant map and listed appropriately. It is not practical for us to quote any indication of quality and cost applicable to hire fleets, and we would recommend that prospective hirers obtain a selection of brochures from bases and agencies of their choice before making a firm booking.

## Boating

Boating on the inland waterways is an established facet of the UK holiday industry. There are over 20,000 privately owned boats registered on the canals and river navigations of Britain. In addition to this there are over a hundred firms offering boats for hire. They range from small operators with half a dozen boats or so to sizeable fleets run by companies with several bases. Size, however, is no barometer of quality. Nowadays most hire boats have all the creature comforts you are likely to require: double beds, showers, flushing loos, fridges, cookers etc etc. Traditionally hire boats are booked out by the week or fortnight, but an increasing number of firms advertise short break holidays of two, three or four days duration; particularly in the Spring and Autumn. All reputable hire firms give newcomers tuition in boat handling, lock working, and general navigation and it's considerably easier than learning to ride a bicycle or drive a car. Whilst a cruise around the Avon Ring would necessarily have to be aboard a narrowboat, anyone restricting their itinerary to the Severn and Avon rivers could avail themselves of a wide beam vessel. Though, it must be said, few hire firms offer such craft, Corsair Cruisers of Upton-on-Severn being a notable example. Whilst Bidford Boats have a delightful Dutch barge available for skippered charter.

## Walking

Towpaths accompany the Stratford and Worcester & Birmingham canals throughout their course. Difficulty of access and poor conditions have been twin factors instrumental in discouraging walkers in the past, but much work has been done to remove such hazards in recent years. British Waterways are currently restoring the towpath of the 'Northern' Stratford Canal which had deteriorated beyond the point of use. There are, however, still sections of towpath on both of these canals which are not conducive to enjoyable walking. The maps show the standard of towpath at any given point. 'Good' can usually be taken to indicate the existence of a firm, wide and dry base; 'adequate' hints at the chance of mud and vegetation, but can usually be considered passable; whilst 'poor' reflects conditions where the towpath has been eroded or become overgrown.

Sadly there is no consistent path beside the River Avon; few rivers have one. Only between Cleeve Prior and Stratford is there a well maintained path open to the public. Upstream of Worcester the Severn is also troublesome to follow. Often what path there is changes sides at the site of an abandoned ferry. In the county of Gloucestershire, however, the 'Severn Way' follows either bank of the river, and is, moreover, admirally signposted.

## Navigational Advice

This Companion consists of canals and river navigations, and the latter, incorporate a number of unusual boating hazards worth considering by those more used to canal cruising.

## Locks.

The locks on the STRATFORD and WORCESTER & BIRMINGHAM canals (except for the pair of wide-beam locks linking Diglis Basin with the River Severn at Worcester) are of standard narrowbeam dimensions and pose no undue difficulties.

The locks on both sections of the RIVER AVON are of widebeam dimensions and capable of taking two narrowboats side by side. Landing stages are provided up and downstream of each chamber to enable boat crews to get off and on their craft. Travelling upstream boats should be secured with lines fore and aft once they are in the lock chamber to prevent them being buffeted by turbulence when the lock fills. On leaving the lock – in either direction – the exit gates may be left open; though do still ensure that the sluices are wound back down. On the LOWER AVON the locks at Tewkesbury, Strensham and Evesham are permanently manned, whilst other locks on the navigation may be operated by volunteer staff during busy periods.

Locks on the RIVER SEVERN are automated. One prolonged blast on the boat horn should be sufficient to alert the keeper that you wish to use the lock if it is apparent that he hasn't seen you arrive. Be guided by the colour light signals, not proceeding too close to the lock chamber until you seen the light is green. The chambers of these locks are disconcertingly large and you may be sharing them with other craft. Steadying chains are fitted to the lock walls and these may be hand held to avoid turbulence. Always follow the lock-keepers advice. The locks operate to a timetable. Hire craft are likely to have up to date details on board. Private owners may acquire copies of "Cruising the Gloucester & Sharpness Canal and River Severn" from British Waterways, Llanthony Warehouse. Gloucester GL1 2EH. Tel: Gloucester (0452) 25524.

*Every lock on the two rivers is shown in an enlargement on the relevant map. Take care to keep to the navigational channel and avoid coming close to the weirs.*

## Moorings.

Mooring on the canals covered by this guide is as per usual – ie on the towpath side away from sharp bends, not in lock flights, bridge holes and narrow sections. Recommended mooring points, of particular relevance to urban areas, are marked on the maps with an open bollard symbol. On the rivers moorings are not so readily available. The banks are either in private ownership or dedicated to fishing rights. Some communities seem to go out of their way to prevent boats from mooring and using their facilities. It seems a perverse attitude in a tourist conscious area, particularly when motorists are given every encouragement to despoil the environment. Reference to the maps will show where it is feasible to moor on the rivers. But bear in mind that facilities are limited. If you see a spot you like and there is a berth free, take it; further on, as night closes in, you may be faced with Hobson's choice. At the height of the season it may be necessary to tolerate mooring side by side with other craft.

## Floods.

The Severn and the Avon are liable to rapid and sudden flooding at any time of the year. Under such conditions boaters can do no other than moor until water levels and current speeds return to normal. On the Avon there is a system of warning signs located beside each lock. Coloured depth gauges also indicate safety levels. Should the river rise while you are on it, locate the nearest safe moorings, remembering to allow sufficient length of mooring line to cope with fluctuations in level: some moorings are provided with sliding rings to accomodate changing levels. If the current is at all strong ensure that you moor with the bows (front) facing upstream. On the River Severn lock-keepers and other BW staff will advise you of flood conditions. Heed their advice and do not attempt to cruise again without their permission. If you are in any doubt at all about flood conditions on either river contact the relevant navigation authority. Boat hire companies will be sympathetic to delays in such circumstances; they are used to the rivers' mercurial moods.

### Speed.

A speed limit of 4mph exists on the Stratford and Worcester & Birmingham canals and on the Upper Avon. On the Lower Avon the limit is 6mph. On the River Severn the limit is 6mph upstream and 8mph downstream. Because boats tend not to be equipped with speedometers these limits tend to be widely interpreted. Moreover a boat travelling at a legal 4mph along a narrow canal can create sizeable waves which do untold damage to the banks. In effect there is only firm rule which should govern your speed, and that is that you should not be making a wash or a wave. It is also considered courteous to slow right down when passing close to moored craft.

### Closures.

Closures (or in waterway parlance: 'stoppages') usually occur between November and April when the bulk of maintenance work is undertaken by the navigation authorities and their sub contractors. Occasionally emergency stoppages take place at short notice and may have repercussions on your itinerary. Up to date details are likely to be available from your hire base. Alternatively, private owners are recommended to contact the relevant authorities before commencing their cruise. British Waterways operate a recorded announcement telephone service, detailing emergency stoppages, read by a young lady with possibly the fastest speaking voice in England. Tel: 01-723 8487 for her latest bravura performance.

## Useful Contacts

British Waterways
Information Centre
Melbury House
Melbury Terrace
London NW1 6JX
01-262 6711

Inland Waterways Association
114 Regent's Park Road
London NW1 8UQ
01-586 2556

Heart of England Tourist Board
2/4 Trinity Street
Worcester WR1 2PW
(0905) 613132

### Acknowledgements

Many thanks to Rob Bell and staff of Viking Afloat for use of a boat for research. All the usual team have made their telling contributions to the production of this guide. The cover, based loosely on Cadbury's old boat livery is by Brian Collings; the frontispiece of Lowesmoor, Worcester – and all other illustrations – are by Eric Leslie. Thanks, as always, to everyone involved at Character Graphics and Penwell Print. Richard Stone was an assistant crew member and Tom & Jeanne Foxon made a welcome cameo appearence. The 'soundtrack' was provided by Ivor Gurney, Eddy Elgar, Van Morrison & Mr Brahms. Our indispensable vade-mecum was the 'Sunlight Soap Year Book for 1898. Mrs Pearson's wardrobe was supplied by B&Q.